DREAM OF REALITY

DREAM OF REALITY

An Evangelical encounters the Oxford Movement

Roger Steer

Hodder & Stoughton
LONDON SYDNEY AUCKLAND

Unless otherwise indicated, Scripture quotations are taken
from The HOLY BIBLE, NEW INTERNATIONAL
VERSION, copyright © 1973, 1978, 1984, By The
International Bible Society.
Extracts from *The Message of the Sermon on the Mount* by
J. R. W. Stott, 1978, IVP, used by permission.

British Library Cataloguing in Publication Data
A Catalogue record for this book is available from
the British Library

ISBN 0-340-56570-5

Published by Hodder and Stoughton,
a division of Hodder and Stoughton Ltd,
Mill Road, Dunton Green, Sevenoaks, Kent TN13 2YA
Editorial Office: 47 Bedford Square, London WC1B 3DP

Typeset by Hewer Text Composition Services, Edinburgh
Printed in Great Britain by Clays Ltd, St Ives plc.

Ex umbris et imaginibus in veritatem
Out of reality into Reality

Words chosen by John Henry Newman
for his memorial tablet at Rednal, near Birmingham

Contents

1   Sunday afternoon at St Mary's

Yesterday, I visited Matthew Arnold's 'sweet city with her dreaming spires'. I walked down the Broad, past the Sheldonian Theatre, into Radcliffe Square and gazed up at the spectacular spire of the University Church which has dominated the Oxford skyline for nearly seven hundred years. In a shower of rain, I took refuge in the church, slipping in through the North Porch, and recalled that in the Middle Ages the university carried on its business in St Mary's. Dons delivered their lectures here, academic disputes were heard, undergraduates sat their exams – and, if they stayed the course, received their degrees in the nave.

I wandered through the university's first little library and into the Old Congregation House where the 'parliament' of the university used to meet, all under the church's roof. I admired the church's light and graceful nave built at the end of the fifteenth century after Henry VII had donated forty oaks from his own land to the east of the town. I inspected Adam de Brome's chapel, a rather dark and dreary place on the north side of the church, which looked more like a court or a place of business than a chapel.

Has anywhere in England, I wondered, experienced a richer slice of history than St Mary's? When, towards the end of the fourteenth century, the teaching of the master of Balliol College, John Wyclif, disturbed the routine of university studies, the church became the focal point for the launch of the Lollard movement which anticipated the English Reformation two hundred years later. Then, in April 1554, three English Reformers – Archbishop Cranmer and Bishops Ridley and Latimer – began to experience their long ordeal of trials here. I looked at Cranmer's pillar

1

and saw where they cut away the moulding to secure a platform on which the Archbishop was condemned for heresy.

Queen Elizabeth I twice visited the church to hear lengthy disputations, as did James I after her. Still later, while the court of Charles I was at Oxford during the Civil War, sermons were preached regularly at St Mary's before both Houses of Parliament.

In the early eighteenth century, the Wesley brothers appeared at Oxford, and John preached eight university sermons in St Mary's – the final one just three weeks after his famous experience in London when he had felt his heart 'strangely warmed' and trusted in Christ alone for salvation.

Ninety years later, in 1827–8, St Mary's underwent a general refitting. They constructed new galleries, erected a stone choir-screen and installed a new pulpit. I looked around the church; the early nineteenth-century additions were still there. I walked over to the pulpit, now one hundred and sixty-five years old, but in splendid condition. Here, on July 14th, 1833, John Keble had stood and preached his Assize sermon in which he defended the rights of the Church against Government interference. With the Church under threat from various quarters, no one, Keble argued, could devote himself too much to the cause of the apostolic Church or to personal devotion and prayer.

Keble's sermon is usually regarded as marking the beginning of the 'Oxford Movement' about which I knew a little. I understood that the movement had stressed the identity of the Church as a divine society, with an apostolic ministry continued through the historic line of bishops, and sacramental worship as the means of grace. I believed that the movement's leaders had seen themselves as working for the renewal of the Church in the face of growing secularism and liberalism.

In the year the new pulpit had been installed, John Henry Newman, another name to become famous in the Oxford

Movement, had become vicar of St Mary's, a post he held until he resigned in 1843. Under Newman's lead, St Mary's became a focal point of the movement and the church's pulpit during the fifteen years of Newman's ministry there exerted a greater influence than at any other time in its momentous history. Dons and undergraduates flocked to hear Newman preach and many of the students copied his mannerisms and imitated every inflexion of his voice. James Mozley, who later became Regius Professor of Divinity at the university, admitted that in his preaching he imitated Newman 'just as an Evangelical preaches in an Evangelical style': he was perhaps the first in a long line of Newmanite preachers.

'Who', Matthew Arnold recalled forty years later, 'could resist the charm of that spiritual apparition, gliding in the dim afternoon light through the aisles of St Mary's, rising into the pulpit, and then, in the most entrancing of voices breaking the silence with words and thoughts which were a religious movement, subtle, sweet, mournful?' Lord Coleridge remembered, 'There was scarcely a man of note in the university, old or young, who did not, during the last two or three years of Newman's incumbency, habitually attend the service and listen to the sermons.'

I turned and looked up to the west gallery at the rear of the church, brand new in Newman's day, and tried to imagine it packed with undergraduates. What was it about Newman which so captivated those young men? What were the insights of the men of the Oxford Movement – Newman, Keble and Pusey – which did so much to revive the spiritual life of the Church of England? How much did their ideas differ from those of Wyclif and Wesley who had occupied an earlier pulpit in this beautiful church? I had heard that Newman and his friends had a deep sense of the mystery of the Christian gospel and of the holiness of God which transcended human language. I knew that Newman through his sermons and Keble through his

3

poetry had powerfully expressed these themes, with a call to holiness – but I was intrigued to know more about the movement.

It was warm in the church and I was tired after my journey from Devon. I sat down on a pew close to Newman's pulpit. Why was it, I wondered, that in the Evangelical circles in which I had grown up, the leaders of the movement had been so rarely quoted in sermons – though we sometimes sang Newman's and Keble's hymns? I remembered reading that someone had described the movement as a period of renewal in the Church of England to which 'the Evangelical movement gave the spirit and the Catholic movement the form'; that though the followers of the two parties in the Church were often locked in fierce public controversies they actually had much in common, as some of them even acknowledged at the time – a shared concern for a religion of the heart.

The St Mary's organist began to play a rather melancholy but strangely beautiful piece of music, presumably rehearsing for a service, and I found it more and more difficult to stay awake. Outside, the shower passed and the sun began to stream through a window in the south aisle which commemorates John Keble. At last, I fell asleep and began to dream.

In my dream I was still in St Mary's but the church was packed with people of all ages. Some I judged to be dons, some undergraduates and some looked as though they might be shopkeepers and tradespeople from the town. As I watched I saw a man in clerical dress walk quickly to a stall beneath the pulpit. He was rather above middle height and very thin; although he didn't stoop he bent slightly forward. His head was large and I quickly recognised the features from a bronze bust I had seen in the garden of Trinity College. It was the Reverend John Henry Newman.

Newman looked like a man who seemed to dwell apart – almost as if he knew the age in which he lived, but

4

wasn't quite a part of it. Even in my dream I remembered the description of a contemporary who wrote that 'from the seclusion of study, and abstinence, and prayer, from habitual dwelling in the unseen, Newman seemed to come forth that one day of the week to speak to others of the things he had seen and known'. And here was I, witnessing the weekly event.

The service was led at first by Newman's curate; it was all very simple – there was no pomp, no ritual. I heard later that all the leading men of the Oxford Movement left elaborate ceremonial to some among their disciples; Newman called mere ritualists 'gilt-gingerbread' men. I soon gathered that the season of the year was Lent.

I shall never forget the reading of the lesson for it was the first time I heard Newman's voice. He read from John 12:20–36 where Jesus predicted His death. I'd never heard such a clear voice – if sounds have a colour, this was of silver and it rang out through the high Gothic church like unearthly music. The pronunciation was so distinct that you could almost count each vowel and consonant in every word. As he read the passage from the Gospel, he seemed to bring new meaning to words which were familiar to me.

I wondered what the theme of Newman's sermon would be. Would we be treated to a powerful proclamation of high church doctrine, an attack on dissenters, perhaps?

Newman began his sermon by reading his text, from John 12:32, 'And I, if I be lifted up from the earth, will draw all men unto me' (AV). He paused, bowed his head for a moment, glanced at the silent congregation and began.

5

2 'Let us begin with Christ'

'A great number of men,' Newman said, 'live and die without
reflecting at all upon the state of things in which they find
themselves. They take things as they come, and follow their
inclinations as far as they have the opportunity. They are
guided mainly by pleasure and pain, not by reason, principle,
or conscience; and they do not attempt to *interpret* this world,
to determine what it means, or to reduce what they see and
feel to system. But when persons, either from thoughtfulness
of mind, or from intellectual activity, begin to contemplate
the visible state of things into which they are born, then they
find it a maze and a complexity. It's a riddle which they cannot
solve. It seems full of contradictions and without a drift. Why
it is, and what it is to issue in, and how it is what it is, and how
we come to be introduced into it, and what is our destiny, are
all mysteries.

'In this difficulty, some have sought one philosophy of life,
and others another. Men have thought they had found the
key, by means of which they might read what is so obscure.
Ten thousand things come before us one after another in the
course of life, and what are we to think of them? What colour
are we to give them? Are we to look at all things in a gay and
mirthful way? Or in a melancholy way? In a despondent or
a hopeful way? Are we to make light of life altogether, or to
treat the whole subject seriously? . . .'

The style of Newman's delivery startled me at first. He
spoke each separate sentence, or at least each short section,
very quickly but still with the very clear intonation which
had marked his reading of the Scripture. But at the end of
each short section, he paused for almost half a minute – and
then spoke more rapid sentences followed by another pause.
It took some time to get used to this, but as I did, I grew
enchanted with the charm of it.

'*How* are we to look at things?' Newman asked, the level
of his sweet musical voice now rising slightly as he warmed

to his theme. 'This is the question which all persons of observation ask themselves, and answer each in his own way. They wish to think by rule; by something within them which may harmonise and adjust what is outside them. This is the need felt by reflective minds.

'Now let me ask, what *is* the real key, what is the Christian interpretation of this world? What is given us by revelation to estimate and measure the world by? The answer is the event of this season – the Crucifixion of the Son of God.

'It is the death of the eternal Word of God made flesh which is our great lesson how to think and how to speak of this world. His cross has put its due value on everything which we see, upon all fortunes, all advantages, all ranks, all dignities, all pleasures; upon the lust of the flesh, and the lust of the eyes, and the pride of life. It has set a price upon the excitements, the rivalries, the hopes, the fears, the desires, the efforts, the triumphs of mortal man.

'The cross has given a meaning to the various, the shifting course, the trials, the temptations, the sufferings of man's earthly state. It has brought together and made consistent all that seemed discordant and aimless. It has taught us how to live, how to use this world, what to expect, what to desire, what to hope. It is the tone into which all the strains of this world's music are ultimately to be resolved.

'Look around and see what the world presents of high and low. Go to the courts of princes. See the treasure and skill of all nations brought together to honour a child of man. Observe the prostration of the many before the few. Consider the form and ceremonial, the pomp, the state, the circumstance; and the vainglory. Do you wish to know the worth of it all? Look at the cross of Christ.'

I glanced around at the packed church. The congregation seemed breathless with expectant attention. Only the gas-light, just to the left of the pulpit, flickered, illuminating a stone angelic figure perched high above the pulpit with arms extended as if in inspiration.

'Go to the political world:' Newman continued, 'see nation

7

jealous of nation, trade rivalling trade, armies and fleets matched against each other. Survey the various ranks of the community, its parties and their contests, the strivings of the ambitious, the intrigues of the crafty. What is the end of all this turmoil? The grave. What is the measure? The cross.

'Go again to the world of intellect and science: consider the wonderful discoveries which the human mind is making, the variety of arts to which the discoveries give rise, the all but miracles by which it shows its power; and next the pride and confidence of reason, and the absorbing devotion of thought to transitory objects which is the consequence. Would you form a right judgment of all this? Look at the cross.

'Look at misery, look at poverty and destitution, look at oppression and captivity; go where food is scanty and lodging unhealthy. Consider pain and suffering, disease long or violent, all that is frightening and revolting. Would you know how to rate all these? Gaze upon the cross.

'Thus in the cross, and Him Who hung upon it, all things meet; all things subserve it, all things need it. It is their centre and their interpretation. For He was lifted up upon it that He might draw all men and all things unto Him.'

Can this be the great high churchman who later became a cardinal? – I wondered. I had expected a more 'churchy' tone, but there was little to distinguish this from a classically Christ-centred Evangelical sermon.

'But it will be said,' Newman continued, 'that the view which the cross of Christ imparts to us of human life and of the world is not that which we should take if left to ourselves; that it is not an obvious view; that if we look at things on the surface they are far more bright and sunny than they appear when viewed in the light which this season of Lent casts upon them. The world seems made for the enjoyment of just such a being as man, and man is put into it. He has the *capacity* for enjoyment, and the world supplies the *means*. How natural this, what a simple as well as pleasant philosophy, yet how different from that of the cross! The doctrine of the cross, it may be said, disarranges two parts of a system which seem made for each other; it severs the fruit from the eater, the enjoyment from the enjoyer. How does this solve the problem? Does it not rather create one?'

Newman answered this question by referring to Adam and Eve in the Garden of Eden, and noting that we too are still in a world where there is forbidden fruit, that our trials lie in being within reach of it, and our happiness in abstaining from it.

'But again,' Newman continued, 'it's a superficial view to say that this life is made for pleasure and happiness. To look under the surface, it tells a very different tale. The doctrine of the cross does teach, though infinitely more forcibly, still after all it does teach the very same lesson which this world teaches to those who live long in it, who have much experience in it, who know it.

'The world is sweet to the lips, but bitter to the taste. It pleases at first but not at last. It looks gay on the outside, but evil and misery lie concealed within. When a man has passed a certain number of years in it he cries out with the Preacher in the Book of Ecclesiastes, "Vanity of vanities, all is vanity" (1:2 AV).

'Therefore the doctrine of the cross of Christ simply anticipates for us our experience of the world. Certainly it bids us grieve for our sins in the midst of all that smiles and glitters around us; but if we will not heed it, we shall at length be forced to grieve for them from undergoing this fearful punishment. If we will not acknowledge that this world has been made miserable by sin, from the sight of Him on Whom our sins were laid, we shall experience it to be miserable by the recoil of those sins upon ourselves.

'We may grant then, that the doctrine of the cross isn't on the surface of the world. The surface of things is bright only, and the cross is sorrowful; it's a hidden doctrine; it lies under a veil; it at first sight startles us, and we are tempted to revolt from it. Like Peter, we cry out, "Never, Lord! This shall never happen to you!" (Matt. 16:22). And yet it's true doctrine; for truth is not on the surface of things, but in the depths.

'And as the doctrine of the cross, though it is the interpretation of this world, isn't prominently manifested in it, upon its surface, but is concealed; so again, when received into the faithful heart, there it abides as a living principle, but deep, and hidden from observation . . .

'And so the great and awful doctrine of the cross of Christ, which we now commemorate, may fitly be called, in the language of figure, the *heart* of religion. The heart may be considered as the seat of life; it is the principle of motion, heat and activity; from it the blood goes to and fro to the extreme parts of the body. It sustains the man in his powers and faculties; it enables the brain to think; and when it is touched, man dies.

'In the same way the sacred doctrine of Christ's atoning sacrifice is the vital principle on which the Christian lives, and without which Christianity is not. Without it no other doctrine is held profitably; to believe in Christ's divinity, or in His manhood, or in the Holy Trinity, or in a judgment to come, or in the resurrection of the dead, is an untrue belief, not a Christian faith, unless we receive also the doctrine of Christ's sacrifice.

'On the other hand, to receive the doctrine of the cross presupposes the reception of other high truths of the gospel besides; it involves the belief in Christ's true divinity, in His true incarnation, and in man's sinful state by nature; and it prepares the way to belief in the sacred eucharistic feast, in which He Who was once crucified is ever given to our souls and bodies in His body and His blood.

'But again, the heart is hidden from view; it is carefully and securely guarded; it isn't like the eye set in the forehead, commanding all, and seen of all: and so in the same way the sacred doctrine of the atoning sacrifice isn't one to be talked of, but to be lived; not to be put forward irreverently, but to be adored secretly; not to be used as a necessary instrument in the conversion of the ungodly, or for the satisfaction of reasoners of this world, but to be unfolded to the docile and obedient; to young children who the world hasn't corrupted; to the sorrowful who need comfort; to the sincere and earnest who need a rule for life; to the innocent who need a warning; and to the established, who have earned the knowledge of it.'

Here's a difference, I thought. This isn't an Evangelical preaching. Wasn't Newman saying that we can't use the doctrine of the atonement in seeking the conversion of sinners? Is this, I wondered, the doctrine of 'Reserve' put forward by the authors of the Oxford Movement's *Tracts for the Times*, that the deepest Christian truth should only be communicated to men and women as by moral growth they are able to receive it?

'I shall make one more remark and then conclude,' Newman said. 'Do not think that because the gospel of the cross makes us sad that therefore the gospel is a sad religion. The Psalmist says, "They that sow in tears shall reap in joy" (Ps. 126:5 AV); and our Lord says, "Blessed are those who mourn, for they will be comforted" (Matt. 5:4). Let no one go away with the impression that the gospel makes us take a gloomy view of the world and of life. It does hinder us from taking a superficial view, and finding a vain transitory joy in what we see; but it forbids our immediate enjoyment, only to grant enjoyment in truth and fullness afterwards. It only forbids us to *begin* with enjoyment. It only says, if you begin with pleasure, you will end in pain. It bids us begin with the cross of Christ, and in that cross we shall find at first sorrow, but in a while peace and comfort will rise out of that sorrow.

'The cross will lead us to mourning, repentance, humiliation, prayer, fasting; we shall sorrow for our sins, we shall sorrow with Christ's sufferings; but all this sorrow will only issue, no, will be undergone in a happiness far greater than the enjoyment which the world gives . . .

'Our Saviour said to His disciples, "Now is your time of grief, but I will see you again and you will rejoice, and no-one will take away your joy" (John 16:22) . . . "Peace I leave with you; my peace I give you. I do not give to you as the world

11

gives" (John 14:27) . . . And thus the cross of Christ, as telling us of our redemption as well as of His sufferings, wounds us indeed, but so wounds as to heal also.

'And thus, too, all that is bright and beautiful, even on the surface of this world, though it has no substance, and may not suitably be enjoyed for its own sake, yet is a figure and promise of that true joy which issues out of the atonement. It is a promise beforehand of what is to be: it is a shadow, raising hope because the substance is to follow, but not to be rashly taken instead of the substance. And it's God's usual mode of dealing with us, in mercy to send the shadow before the substance, that we may take comfort in what is to be, before it comes.'

Newman went on to give some illustrations of this principle of shadow preceding substance from the final weeks of the life of Christ. Then he concluded, 'And so too, as regards this world with all its enjoyments, yet disappointments. Let us not trust it; let us not give our hearts to it; let us not begin with it. Let us begin with faith; let us begin with Christ; let us begin with His cross and the humiliation to which it leads. Let us first be drawn to Him who is lifted up, that so He may, with Himself, freely give us all things (Rom. 8:32). Let us "seek first his kingdom and his righteousness" and then all those things of this world "will be given to you as well" (Matt. 6:33).

'They alone are able truly to enjoy this world who begin with the world unseen. They alone enjoy it who have first abstained from it. They alone can truly feast who have first fasted; they alone are able to use the world who have not learned to abuse it; they alone inherit it who take shelter in the world to come, and who for that world to come relinquish it.'

Newman returned quietly to his stall. I had found his sermon moving, inspiring, challenging – but puzzling. I loved the centrality Newman had given to the cross, but was disturbed to hear him say, if I had rightly understood him, that the doctrine of the atonement shouldn't be used explicitly

12

in seeking the conversion of sinners. I was convinced though that no one could come away from listening to this sermon without feeling ashamed of coarseness, selfishness, frivolity or worldliness.

3   Tom Mozley

Immediately after the service I had what I might call a stroke of luck except that, having sat through Newman's sermon, it seemed more appropriate to think of it as a fortunate encounter: I found myself talking to the Rev. Tom Mozley.

Mozley turned out to be married to Newman's sister Harriet, and a former Fellow of Oriel College, the college of which Newman was still a Fellow. He was rector of Plymtree in Devon and when he discovered that I was myself on a visit from Devon he began to talk expansively and colourfully. I gathered from Mozley that the year was 1842. Nothing in my appearance apparently suggested to Mozley that I was an apparition visiting Oxford from the late twentieth century – and I don't remember that in my dream it occurred to me that he should detect anything odd about me.

'I must admit,' Mozley told me with a twinkle in his eye, 'that although I'm Newman's brother-in-law, whenever I return to Oxford for a visit, I feel that my incurable worldliness clashes with the serious and saintly tone of the movement which he represents.'

'I know less than I should about the Oxford Movement,' I told Mozley, 'being from an Evangelical background myself. I was certainly inspired by the tone of your brother-in-law's sermon, but found parts of it puzzling.'

I hesitated to go on, wondering whether Mozley would even be familiar with the term 'Evangelical' or whether it had the same meaning in the 1840s as it has in the 1990s.

'Well, if you would care to come with me,' Mozley continued, 'you can perhaps put your questions to Newman.

13

I am due to meet him later this afternoon. He also grew up among Evangelicals, as indeed I did. We won't go straight to his rooms at Oriel, though, as he doesn't care for company immediately after a service.'

Mozley and I began to walk through the streets of Oxford, talking as we walked.

'How do you characterise the typical Evangelical preacher?' I asked, hoping that his answer would reveal whether the term had changed its meaning without indicating to Mozley that he was talking to someone from another age.

'The Evangelical clergyman,' Mozley replied, 'assumes that the great mass of people committed to his care are utterly bad or hopelessly good.'

'What do you mean, "hopelessly good"?' I interrupted.

'I mean that the Evangelical clergyman thinks they are hopelessly trusting in good works. The utterly bad and the hopelessly good he can discard altogether from his consideration. He has delivered his message and that is enough for him. He can then reserve his attention for a few, and will naturally consult his tastes and preferences in their selection. Relieved from the dull round of house-to-house work performed by the high churchman, and from close parochial duty generally, he becomes mobilised.

'He goes around preaching and hearing preaching; he speaks from platforms and hears speeches; he comes across missionaries, philanthropists, and the travelling staff of societies. He sees something of the wealthier and more educated people than may live in his own parish. He's in the world, and every day he acquires more and more of that knowledge and of those manners that in the world make the difference between one man and another.

'The Evangelical preacher soon discovers that his vocation is not in cottages or hovels, or in farm-houses, or in garrets and cellars, in dirty lanes and courts. These clergymen are known, while the others are unknown. Evangelical preachers are announced and paraded. The corners of the streets and the newspapers proclaim their appointments and invite listeners

14

from all quarters. They seek the most roomy and best situated churches and, long before the Oxford Movement, rich patrons were quickly buying up the most important pulpits for them.'

'I think you're being very cynical,' I ventured rashly, considering my own relative ignorance of the nineteenth-century Church scene, 'but I suppose I do recognise something in what you say from my own experience. Tell me what you think of the sermons Evangelicals preach.'

'The doctrine they preach is simple enough,' Mozley continued, warming to his task, and apparently not offended by my censure. 'The fortunate discoverers and propagators of their Evangelical doctrine rejoice in its simplicity. Simple, for it excludes everything else. You are to be quite sure not only that you have received a special revelation that Jesus Christ died for you in particular, but also that your salvation is now a certainty which places you above all further anxiety. You might have your faults, but you are saved. Your neighbours might have their virtues, but, lacking this personal assurance, they aren't saved. They're not even one step on the way to salvation.'

'You sound as if you've a good deal of personal experience of this type of preaching,' I said.

'Well, I sat under it for many years as a boy and as a teenager in Derby, indeed right up to my ordination whenever I returned home from Oxford. So I'm sure that my impressions are well founded. Actually I like some of the Evangelical preachers personally and greatly respect others whom I don't know so well.

'However, I must say that the impression of the Evangelical system on my mind after hearing thousands of such sermons is this: it pays too little attention to the character and teachings of Jesus Christ. It reduces the Sermon on the Mount, all the discourses of our Lord, and all the moral arguments and exhortations of Paul and the other apostles to mere carnalities that no real Christian need have anything to do with. These passages of Scripture consciously

15

or subconsciously are thought of as mere moralising – not the gospel.

'All that is tender, all that is touching, all that appeals to our higher and noble feelings, all that by which Jesus Christ is the object of unbounded love and adoration even to those who shrink from the attempt to fathom the mystery of His being are thrown aside, trampled upon, as likely to lead us astray from the real point at issue, that is, whether we ourselves are personally saved to our own certain knowledge.'

'What do you think is the effect of this sort of preaching?' I asked.

'Well, hundreds of times I have looked round on a congregation to see how they are reacting to the final and irreversible sentence of eternal doom sounded continually in their ears. As often as not everybody is asleep, except a few too stupid to be ever quite awake or quite asleep. Humanity and common sense revolt against these sermons and they can really no more reach the understanding than so many letters of the alphabet shaken out of a bag upon a table.'

'Aren't you being very harsh?' I asked. I felt a sense of confused loyalty towards many delightful people I have known. I wasn't sure whether Mozley had treated me to an unfair caricature of Evangelical preaching or whether Evangelical preachers had become more mature in their understanding of the gospel over one and a half centuries. But I knew that I had heard similar sermons preached. Mozley either didn't hear my question, or chose not to answer.

'So how do you describe the typical high church clergyman?' I asked.

'Well,' Mozley replied, 'you can see the high churchman every day in his parish; he is visiting sick folk or calling on the gentlefolk. In the streets and lanes he meets everyone and exchanges a word with them. He never seems especially busy or in a hurry; he never looks as if he's rushing to keep an appointment, booked for a meeting, or on his way to a coach-office. He may sometimes seem idle and even too accessible. But you can always see him. If you want to, you can talk to him; and if you want more, you can have a serious talk.

'Compared with his ordinary parishioners he's well read. Sometimes he'll be polemic in what he says – he may even be a peppery polemic. He won't know what to do about dissenters and will perhaps sound peevish in his expressions about them.

'On Sundays he'll deliver a cut-and-dried sermon; if he's a big fellow with a strong voice, *ore rotundo*; if not, in a monotonous tone almost as if to admit that what he's saying is hardly worth your attention. Yet there are some very good and energetic high church preachers.

'The high church clergyman is normally a good pastor. The two things go together naturally because, as a high churchman, he assumes everyone in his parish to be his flock, all to be Christians on the road to heaven, though requiring much help, guidance and stimulus.

'Of course he has to work quietly. There's no one to report or publish his talk. His best things are said to one at a time. A hard day's work won't be known even in the next parish. Talking every day with poor country people he becomes more or less like them, for we all grow like those we're most with.'

Mozley and I had now reached Christ Church meadow, the large grassy area where cows still graze today in the shadow of the cathedral and which stretches down to the point where the River Cherwell joins the Thames.

'Whenever I reach the meadows,' said Mozley, who seemed to want to change the conversation to a lighter subject, 'I think of Richard Whately. He was a contemporary of mine at Oriel and a Fellow there until 1831 when he became Archbishop of Dublin. He enormously influenced Newman's thinking. His rough manners, huge frame, vast helpings at high table, were notorious at the university. He smoked many pipes, wore untidy clothes and looked nothing like a clergyman. He rarely read books except to dwell on five or six favourite authors. He loved to battle out his ideas in the rough and tumble of vigorous conversation.

'People called him "the white bear" and early in the morning you could see him walking across Christ Church meadows wearing a white hat on the back of his head and dressed in a rough white coat, stone-coloured trousers, and flesh-coloured stockings. He'd be surrounded by a little company of dogs and would throw sticks and big round missiles for their amusement. He used to lecture to an awkward squad of elderly undergraduates at St Alban Hall (where Newman was his vice-principal for a while) lying on a sofa with one leg over the back or the end.

'Now Whately regarded high churchmen and low churchmen as equally bigoted. To him, Evangelical Christianity was a system of dogmas framed to create a groundless self-confidence, and to foster spiritual pride. Whately had little time for the man who was inwardly sure of his own salvation and of his Christian sufficiency, and equally sure of the damnation of most people around him. Such a man, to Whately, wasn't interested in further knowledge and improvement being as good as he thought he needed to be; indeed the only danger, this sort of man believed, was of being so good as to rely on his own merits.'

Fortunately, I thought, you don't meet many Evangelicals like that today. I had no way of knowing to what extent Mozley's colourful descriptions of the Christian world of his own time, and the views he attributed to Whately, were accurate.

'Although Whately sympathised with the Evangelicals' disdain for church formularies, and even for Creeds,' Mozley told me, 'he had still less respect for them than he had for old fashioned high churchmen who at least were well read and cultivated and appealed to something beyond those incommunicable sensations which it was impossible to reason about.'

We were now approaching Oriel College.

'Do you know Oriel?' Mozley asked.

'No.'

'In 1800, Oriel became the first college to throw open its fellowships for competition by examination; then, if I may say this modestly, in the second and third decades of this century, a fellowship at the college was the highest distinction a man could attain. The list of Fellows included the most distinguished names in the university: Whately, Keble, Newman, Arnold, Pusey, Hampden, Davison, Tyler, Hawkins, Dorford, Awdry, Copleston and Jelf.

'Examiners for an Oriel Fellowship don't so much look for evidence of wide reading in history and philosophy as for two things: a man's skill in languages and ability to think for himself. There's a certain prejudice against a man who seems to be trying to be flashy, or show off his reading, especially if, in so doing, he shows that he doesn't know how to make good use of what he's read.

'It's an attractive college, though much smaller than Trinity or Christ Church. They say that to belong to the Oriel common room is an education in itself. I suppose the distinctive feature of the Oriel mind is exactness of thought as the basis of accuracy of expression. Dons practise the Socratic method of refining thought by constant cross-questioning. Fine words are discouraged if homely expressions can make the point.

'When I came up to the college at Easter, 1825,' Mozley continued, cheerfully, 'one of the standing jokes against the college, all over the university, was the "Oriel teapot", which was supposed to be always ready – the centre of the Oriel circle, and its special inspiration. Wherever I went, when I passed the wine, I was asked whether I wouldn't prefer some tea, much to the amusement of the table.'

We arrived at the front quad at Oriel.

'Stop,' said Mozley, 'can you hear him?'

I looked blank.

'Newman's playing his violin. Did you know that he's a keen violinist? I've often heard him play in a quartet in his rooms. I can remember contrasting the expression on his face with one of the other players – a man named Blanco White, who shocked Newman later by becoming a

19

Unitarian. Blanco White always had an excited and agitated look on his face while Newman's expression was always one of sphinxlike immobility.

'Those are his rooms, on the first floor near the chapel. From his bedroom he can go into the gallery of the chapel.'

Mozley pointed up to a huge bay window over the chapel door which balanced what he told me was the dining-hall window.

'Strangers coming to Oxford who want to see where the man who's so stirring the Church of England lives,' Mozley told me, 'are often surprised to find that he simply has an undergraduate's rooms. He shares the same staircase with four undergraduates.'

Tom Mozley and I climbed the staircase together.

4   Newman remembers

We found Newman sitting at a small desk and still holding his violin. The room looked reasonably comfortable and in the middle was a table covered with books and papers. Between two windows which looked out into Merton Lane hung some engravings of St Christopher and three different portraits of Charles the First. Mozley told me later that Newman had scarcely ever put anything new into his rooms since he had taken them over, ready furnished, from his predecessor. One of the indispensable items he treasured, though, was a clean towel always handy, to dust any book which had stayed long on its shelf.

'Mr Steer is from Devon,' Mozley said. 'He has moved among Evangelicals and was both inspired and puzzled by your sermon this afternoon.'

Newman smiled.

'Welcome to Oxford,' he said.

Newman's hair was blacker and longer than it had seemed in St Mary's and his spectacles more prominent.

After Mozley had given Newman news of his sister, I remember asking him about his upbringing.

'I was brought up,' Newman told me, 'to take a great delight in reading my Bible. But I had no real religious convictions until I was fifteen. At that age (in the autumn of 1816) I began to think very differently. I fell under the influence of a definite Creed and received into my intellect impressions of dogma which God has never allowed to be erased.

'The man who influenced me by his sermons and conversations was the Rev. Walter Mayers, of Pembroke College here at Oxford. He was the man God used to begin a divine faith in me; he also lent me books in the school of Calvin which greatly influenced me. One of the first of these books was by Romaine, although I can't remember the title or much about the contents, except for one doctrine which I don't now believe to be from God – that is, the Calvinist doctrine of final perseverance.'

'Do you mean the doctrine that once you're saved, you're always saved?' I asked.

'Yes. I accepted it for a while, and believed that the inward conversion of which I was conscious (and of which I am still more certain than that I have hands and feet) would last into the next life, and that I was elected to eternal glory. I don't think this belief tended to make me careless about pleasing God. I retained the doctrine until I was twenty-one, and then it gradually faded away. I think that this doctrine had some influence on my early opinions in that it isolated me from objects which surrounded me and confirmed me in a distrust of the reality of material phenomena. The doctrine made me rest in the thought of two and only two absolute and luminously self-evident beings, myself and my Creator.

'One Evangelical writer who greatly influenced me as a young man was Thomas Scott. I so admired and delighted in Scott's writings that when I was an undergraduate I thought of making a visit to his parsonage. However, to my dismay, he died before I ever made the trip. I hung upon the lips of the Evangelical preacher Daniel Wilson, later Bishop of Calcutta, when in two sermons at St John's Chapel he told the story of Scott's life and death.

'I think that any reader of Scott's writings would be struck by his bold unworldliness and vigorous independence of mind. He followed truth wherever it led him, beginning with Unitarianism and ending in a zealous faith in the Holy Trinity. It was Scott who first planted in my mind that fundamental truth of religion – the doctrine of the Trinity.

'As well as his unworldliness,' Newman continued, 'what I liked about Scott was his resolute opposition to Antinomianism and the minutely practical character of his writings.'

When I am wide awake I have some difficulty in calling to mind the definition of theological terms, but find this even more difficult in a dream. Newman seemed to sense that he was in danger of losing me.

'Antinomianism,' he said, helpfully, 'so stresses Christian freedom from condemnation of the law that it under-emphasises the need of the believer to confess sin daily and to pursue sanctification earnestly.

'Calvinists,' Newman continued, 'make a sharp separation between the elect and the world. There's much in this which is parallel to Catholic doctrine; but as I understand them, Calvinists go on to say something very different from Catholicism – that we can tell the difference between the converted and the unconverted, that the justified are conscious of their state of justification, and, as I was saying, that the regenerate can't fall away.'

'And what do Catholics say?' I asked.

'Catholics shade and soften the awful antagonism between good and evil, which is one of their dogmas, by holding that there are different degrees of justification, that there's a great difference in point of gravity between sin and sin, that there's no certain knowledge given to any one that he's simply in a state of grace, and much less that he is to persevere to the end.

'Of the Calvinist doctrines the only one which took root in my mind was the fact of heaven and hell, divine favour and

22

divine wrath, of the justified and the unjustified. I didn't retain the Calvinistic notion that the regenerate and the justified were one and the same or, as I have said, that the regenerate as such had the gift of perseverance.

'Also ever since my teenage days I have always believed the doctrine of eternal punishment, as delivered by our Lord Himself, in as true a sense as I hold that of eternal happiness; however I have tried in various ways to make the truth less terrible to the imagination.'

I remembered that in his *Grammar of Assent* Newman had developed the idea that eternity needn't involve the consciousness of the duration of endless time.

'I must mention two other works,' he continued, 'which made a deep impression on me in the autumn of 1816, when I was fifteen years old – books which were contrary to each other and which therefore planted in me the seeds of an intellectual inconsistency which handicapped my thinking for many years.

'I read Joseph Milner's *Church History* and was delighted with his long extracts from St Augustine, St Ambrose and the other Fathers which I found there. I read them as being the religion of the primitive Christians. But at the same time as I read Milner, I read Newton *On the Prophecies*, and as a result became firmly convinced that the Pope was the Antichrist predicted by Daniel, St Paul and St John. The effects of this idea stained my imagination for many years.

'It was also in the autumn of 1816 that I became convinced it was God's will that I should lead a single life. I've felt this ever since – with a few breaks for a month or so until 1829 – but since then without any break at all. I believed that my calling in life would require the sort of sacrifice which celibacy involved: for instance, overseas missionary work to which I felt much drawn for some years. This strengthened my feeling of separation from the visible world of which I've spoken.

'In 1822 I came under new influences, particularly Dr

Whately, who later became Archbishop of Dublin, and who was very kind to me at this time.'

'Mr Mozley painted a vivid picture of Whately to me earlier,' I said.

Newman smiled at his brother-in-law and then at me.

'Well, when he became Principal of St Alban Hall in 1825, Whately made me his vice-principal and tutor. I'll tell you more about him later, but between 1822 and 1825 I saw most of the present Provost of Oriel College, Dr Hawkins, who was then the vicar of St Mary's. When I took orders in 1824 and had a curacy in Oxford, I was thrown into his company a great deal. I can tell you that I love Hawkins and have never ceased to love him. I say this despite the fact that from time to time he provoked me much, and I'm sure that I provoked him even more. In the first years that I knew him he helped in the development of my mind.'

'How did Hawkins affect you at that time?' I asked.

'He was the first person,' Newman replied, 'who taught me to weigh my words, and to be cautious in my statements. He's a man with a very precise mind himself, and he snubbed me severely when he kindly read the first sermon that I wrote and some other essays.

'As to doctrine, he added to my beliefs in many ways. He gave me a copy of the *Treatise on Apostolic Preaching*, by Sumner, which led me to give up my remaining Calvinism and to accept the doctrine of baptismal regeneration – that God saves us by baptism. In many other ways, too, he broadened my mind. Dr Hawkins also taught me to expect that before long, attacks would be made on the books and canon of Scripture.

'One other principle that I gained from Hawkins was the doctrine of Church tradition. When I was an undergraduate, I heard him preach in the university pulpit his celebrated sermon on this subject and it made a great impression on me. His proposition, which is self-evident to those who have seriously examined the structure of Scripture, was that the sacred text was never intended to teach doctrine, but only to prove it, and that, if we would learn doctrine, we must go to the formularies of the Church such as the catechism or the creeds. He believes that, after learning from the doctrines of Christianity, the enquirer must verify them by Scripture. This view is true in its outline, fruitful in its consequences, and opened up for me a large field of thought.

'In about the year 1823, the Rev. William James, then Fellow of Oriel, taught me the doctrine of apostolic succession during the course of a walk around Christ Church meadow. I now saw that, while on the Continent Reformers had for the most part abandoned the ancient concept of the Church as a visible body, in England this wasn't the case. Here it remained the Body of Christ, linked through apostolic succession of the bishops with the apostles and with our Lord, Who commissioned them. In one of our collects we say that God Himself has "built His Church upon the foundation of the apostles and prophets, Jesus Christ being the head corner stone".

'Also at this time, I read Bishop Butler's *Analogy* which was, as it has been to so many people, a landmark in my religious thought. In this he speaks of a visible Church, the oracle of truth and a pattern of sanctity, of the duties of external religion, and of the historical character of revelation.'

As it happened, I was at that time reading through Butler's *Analogy*, but as Newman was now in full flow I decided not to mention it.

'Returning to Dr Whately,' Newman said, 'I can tell you that I owe him a great deal. While I was awkward and timid he took me by the hand and became a gentle and encouraging instructor. He opened my mind, taught me to think and use my reason, to see with my own eyes and walk with my own feet. But his mind was too different from mine for us to remain long in agreement.

'I must confess that at this time I was beginning to prefer intellectual excellence to moral and that I was drifting in the direction of the liberalism of the day. I'm glad to say that I didn't remain a liberal for long.

'During the first years of my residence at Oriel, though I

was proud of my college, I wasn't quite at home there. I was very much alone, and I often used to take my daily walk by myself. From 1823, I enjoyed the friendship of my dear and true friend Dr Pusey. Perhaps you'll meet him while you're in Oxford. I couldn't help admiring a soul so devoted to the cause of religion, so full of good works and so faithful in his affections. Apart from Pusey, there was no one in Oxford to whom in the early years I really opened my heart.

'But things changed in 1826. I became one of the tutors of my college and this gave me position. I wrote one or two essays which were well received. I began to be known. I preached my first university sermon. I became one of the public examiners for the BA degree. In 1828 I became vicar of St Mary's. It was to me like the feeling of spring weather after winter; I came out of my shell.'

5 Origins of a movement

'What were the origins of the Oxford Movement?' I asked Newman.

'The real author of the movement was John Keble,' Newman replied. 'As a mere boy, Keble had carried off the highest honours of this university and his was the first name I heard spoken of with reverence when I came up to Oxford. I remember walking in the High Street with a friend and he cried out, "There's Keble!" and with what awe I looked at him! However when I was elected a Fellow of Oriel in 1822 he wasn't in residence, and he was shy of me for years because of the marks I bore of both Evangelical and liberal schools of thought.

'Keble wrote his *Christian Year* in 1827 and this has of course become a classic of the English language. When the general tone of religious literature was nerveless and impotent, Keble struck an original note with religious teaching which was deep, pure and beautiful. His writing brought home to me what may be called, in a large sense of the word, the sacramental system: that is the doctrine that material phenomena are both the types and the instruments of real things unseen. Keble heightened my awareness of the mysteries of the Christian faith.

'Another key figure in the birth of the Oxford Movement was Hurrell Froude, a pupil of Keble's, who grew up in the county where you come from. I first met him in 1826, and was a very close friend until his death from tuberculosis in 1836. He was a man who combined the highest gifts with a gentle and tender nature; he was playful, versatile of mind, patient in discussion.

'Froude was brimful and overflowing with original ideas and views which were too many and strong for his own bodily strength: his ideas crowded and jostled against each other in their attempt to arrive at shape and expression. His intellect was critical, logical, speculative and bold. His opinions arrested and influenced me, even when I didn't agree with them.

'Though he remained an Anglican until he died, Froude professed his admiration of the Church of Rome and his disdain for the Reformers. He scorned the maxim, "The Bible and the Bible only is the religion of Protestants"; and he gloried in accepting tradition as a main instrument of religious teaching. He had a severe idea of the intrinsic excellence of virginity; and he considered the Blessed Virgin Mary its great pattern.

'Froude loved to think of the saints; he had a vivid appreciation of the idea of sanctity, its possibility and its heights; and he was inclined to believe in the occurrence of miracles in the early and middle ages. He accepted the principle of penance and mortification. He had a deep devotion – not to transubstantiation – but to what is called the "real presence" of our Lord in the bread and wine at the sacrament of the Lord's Supper.

'I should say,' Newman told me, 'that Froude's power of entering into the minds of others didn't equal his other gifts;

he couldn't accept, for example, that at that time I really held the Roman Church to be antichristian. On many points he insisted that I agreed with him when I didn't. He didn't seem to understand my difficulties, but he gradually led me to believe in the doctrine of the real presence.

'I can't remember when I first came to look upon antiquity – the writings of the early Fathers of the undivided Church – as the true exponent of the doctrines of Christianity and the basis of the Church of England. I think the works of Bishop Bull were my chief introduction to this principle.

'Some portions of the teaching of the Fathers, magnificent in themselves, came like music to my inward ear, as if they were the response to ideas which, with little external to encourage them, I had long cherished. These ideas were based on the mystical or sacramental principle, and spoke of the various dispensations of the eternal. I understood these passages to mean that the exterior world, physical and historical, was but the manifestation to our senses of realities greater than itself. Nature was a parable. Scripture was an allegory. Pagan literature, philosophy, and mythology, properly understood, were but a preparation for the gospel.'

'What,' I asked, 'were the developments in the secular and religious world which were the background to the rise of the Oxford Movement?'

'During the 1820s and 1830s,' Newman replied, 'great events were happening at home and abroad. Shortly before, there'd been a revolution in France; the French royal family had been dismissed: I held that it was unchristian for nations to cast off their governors, and, much more, sovereigns who had the divine right of inheritance.

'The great agitation for the reform of the House of Commons was going on all around us. The Whigs had come into power; Lord Grey had told the bishops to put their house in order, and some prelates had been insulted and threatened in the streets of London.

'The vital question was, how were we to keep the Church from being liberalised? The Evangelicals seemed to have lost that simplicity and unworldliness which I admired so much in Milner and Scott. It wasn't that I didn't venerate some of the leading men among them, but I must admit that I thought little of Evangelicals as a party. I thought they played into the hands of the liberals.'

'Why had you come to think less of Evangelicals?' I asked.

'I had come to see many Evangelical sermons as hurtful in their rudeness, irreverence and, at times, almost profaneness. They made a most sacred doctrine like the atonement a subject of vehement tirades, or an instrument to excite people's feelings, or a topic for rather vague, general statements in technical language. I felt uncomfortable when I heard our Lord's name and work used as a sort of charm or spell to convert men, not in the self-abasement of prayer and praise, but in the middle of rhetorical flourishes.

'I still looked hopefully towards a number of Evangelicals among whom you could find some of the highest and noblest elements of the Christian character. But I noticed that the children of Evangelical parents, when they saw the world, often became liberals. Children and young people who have grown up on the receiving end of intensive Evangelical preaching become worn out, like a constitution which has undergone some dreadful disease, or an even more dreadful remedy. Give them education and they often become scoffers. I believe Bishop Butler was right when he said that, "Children who are taught, since they were weaned, to rely on the Christian atonement, and in whose ears have been dinned the motives of gratitude to it, etc, before their hearts are trained to understand them, are deadened to them by the time they are twenty-one".'

I wasn't happy with this and hoped to raise with Newman again the subject of Evangelicals and the atonement compared with his own view of the matter.

'I compared that fresh vigorous power, of which I was reading, in the first centuries,' Newman continued, 'with a divided and threatened establishment in the nineteenth century. I thought that if liberalism once got a footing within the Church of England, it was sure of a victory. It seemed to me that Reformation principles were powerless to help the Church of England.

'As to the high church and the low church, I thought that neither had much more of a logical basis than the other. I had now come to have a thorough contempt for the controversial position of the low church. I thought the apostolic form of doctrine was essential and the grounds of evidence for it impregnable. I was supremely confident of the strength of my position and my manner at this time was often a mixture of fierceness and playfulness. I dare say I offended many and I don't want to defend my behaviour.

'Our battle, when the movement began, was with liberalism; by liberalism I mean the anti-dogmatic principle and its developments. From the age of fifteen, dogma has been a fundamental principle of my religion: I know no other religion; I cannot enter into the idea of any other sort of religion; religion as a mere sentiment is to me a dream and a mockery. This was a fundamental principle of the movement which began in 1833.

'We were confident in the truth of a certain definite religious teaching, based upon this foundation of dogma: that is, that there was a visible Church, with sacraments and rites which are the channels of God's grace. I thought that this was the doctrine of Scripture, of the early Church and of the Anglican Church.'

'What,' I asked, 'were your hopes for the Anglican Church during the period that the *Tracts for the Times* were being written by the leaders of the Oxford Movement?'

'I thought that the state of Anglican divinity was something like this,' Newman replied. 'The most vigorous, the clearest, the most fertile minds had through God's mercy been employed in the service of the Anglican Church: minds, too, which were reverent and holy, well instructed both in Scripture and the writings of the Fathers as well as being intellectually gifted. I thought we needed to thank God for that; the original principles of the gospel and the Church had been patiently brought to light.

'But one thing was lacking: Anglican champions and teachers had lived in stormy times – the Reformation and its aftermath; political and other influences had acted upon them in various ways. I thought we had a vast inheritance, but no inventory of our treasures. Everything had been given in profusion; we needed to catalogue, sort, distribute, select, harmonise and complete. We met with truths overstated or misdirected, matters of detail understood in different ways, facts incompletely proved or applied, and rules inconsistently urged or discordantly interpreted.

'So what I thought we needed for our Church's well-being was not invention, nor originality, nor sagacity, nor even learning in our divines; what we needed in the first place was sound judgment, patient thought, discrimination, a comprehensive mind, an abstinence from all private fancies and caprices and personal tastes – in a word, divine wisdom.

'In the years 1834 to 1836, I wrote about the doctrine of the *Via Media* – the idea that Anglicanism steers a middle course between Roman Catholicism and Protestantism. *Via Media* is an expressive title, but not altogether satisfactory because it's at first sight negative. This was my reason for disliking the word "Protestant", that is that it didn't denote the profession of any particular religion at all, and was compatible with infidelity. A *Via Media* was just a receding from extremes – therefore I thought it needed to be drawn out into a definite shape and character: before it could claim our respect it needed to be shown to be one, intelligible and consistent.

'As to what is called the Evangelical religion, I thought that it had no intellectual basis; no internal idea, no principle of unity, no theology. Its adherents had a remarkable propensity to separate from one another. Evangelical theology had no straightforward view on any point – and to hide its poverty it had dressed itself up in a maze of words. I thought that its natural end was liberalism; and the object of the Oxford Movement was to withstand the liberalism of the day. I

31

didn't think that the Evangelical religion was well equipped in this battle.

'The starting point of my faith is of course the being of God. This is as certain to me as the certainty of my own existence, though when I try to put the grounds of that certainty into logical shape I find it difficult. I look out of myself into the world of men, and there I see a sight which fills me with unspeakable distress. The world seems to give the lie to that great truth of which my whole being is so full; and the effect upon me is in consequence as confusing as if it denied that I exist myself. If I looked into a mirror and didn't see my face, I should have the sort of feeling which actually comes upon me when I look into this busy world and see no reflection of its Creator. Were it not for this voice, speaking so clearly in my conscience and my heart, I should be an atheist, or a pantheist, or a polytheist when I looked into the world.'

'But what do you think about all the classic proofs of the existence of God?' I asked.

'I certainly don't deny,' Newman replied, 'the real force of the arguments in proof of a God drawn from the general facts of human society and the course of history, but these don't warm me or enlighten me; they don't take away the winter of my desolation, or make the buds unfold and the leaves grow within me, and make my moral being rejoice.

'Looking at the world around us, I can only say that either there's no Creator, or this living society of men is in a true sense discarded from His presence. If I saw a boy of good make and mind, with the tokens on him of a refined nature, cast upon the world without provision, unable to say whence he came, his birth-place or his family connections, I should conclude that there was some mystery connected with his history, and that he was one of whom, from one cause or other, his parents were ashamed. This would be the only way I could account for the contrast between the promise and the condition of his being.

'And so I argue about the world – *if* there is a God, *since* there is a God, the human race is implicated in some terrible inherited calamity. It's out of joint with the purposes of its Creator. This is a fact, a fact as true as the fact of its existence; and thus the doctrine of what is theologically called original sin becomes to me almost as certain as that the world exists, and as the existence of God.

'In the anarchical world in which we live, I believe that Scripture, though divine, is inadequate on its own to maintain religious truth. Experience proves surely that the Bible doesn't answer a purpose for which it was never intended. It may be accidentally the means of the conversion of individuals; but a book, after all, can't make a stand against the wild, living, intellect of man.

'A power, possessed of infallibility in religious teaching, is happily adapted to be a working instrument in the course of human affairs for smiting hard and throwing back the immense energy of the aggressive, capricious, untrustworthy intellect.

'The historic Christian Church has always proclaimed with energetic clarity the fundamental truths which explain her mission in the world and give a character to her work. She doesn't teach that human nature is irreclaimable – rather that it's to be extricated, purified, and restored. The Church doesn't say that human nature is a mere mass of hopeless evil, but that it has the promise upon it of great things, and even now, in its present state of disorder and excess, it has a virtue and a praise proper to itself.

'But the Church also knows and preaches that such a restoration as she aims at effecting in the world must be brought about, not simply through certain outward provisions of preaching and teaching, but from an inward spiritual power or grace imparted directly from God, and of which she is the channel.

'The Church has it in her charge to rescue human nature from its misery, but not simply by restoring it on its own level, but by lifting it up to a higher level than its own. She recognises in human nature real moral excellence though degraded, but she can't set it free from earth except by exalting it towards heaven. This is why a renovating grace was put into her hands; and the Church insists that all true conversion must begin with the first springs of thought, and to teach that each individual man must be in his own person one whole and perfect temple of God, while he is also one of the living stones which build up a visible religious community.

'"You must be born again" is the simple, direct form of words which the Church uses following her divine Master: "your whole nature must be reborn; your passions, and your affections, and your aims, and your conscience, and your will, must all be bathed in a new element, and reconsecrated to your Maker – and the last, not the least, your intellect"'.

After Newman had talked to me for a little over an hour, I got the impression that Mozley thought we'd taken up enough of his brother-in-law's time. Newman had spoken with obvious sincerity and conviction about the abandonment of his early Evangelical beliefs. But I wanted to hear more about how he and his friends thought, and what they believed, before I would be prepared to consider following them down the same road – not that Newman had been speaking to me like a man who was striving to make a convert.

'I want you to come with me to Balliol College,' Mozley said to me when Newman left the room, 'to meet one of the most colourful figures in Oxford, William Ward. We'll see Newman again tomorrow. But if Newman has puzzled you, I can guarantee that Ward will shock you. But he'll amuse you, too. I'll tell you about him as we walk to Balliol.'

6 Luther's legacy

'William Ward,' Mozley told me as we walked past the Radcliffe Camera in the direction of the Broad, 'is one of the most genial men I've ever known. I think you'll find him delightful company even if you don't agree with his rather extreme views. He's a huge favourite with the college servants at Balliol for whom he always has a friendly word. He loves to recite mock-heroic verses in Latin and English – verses he composed when he was at Winchester. Recently, he was walking back to Balliol from Littlemore in the twilight with Benjamin Jowett and serenaded his companion with songs from *Don Giovanni*! He knows all the operas.

'Ward's very much a Balliol man, a Fellow of the college, a great name in the university. He represents unanswerable logic and exudes self-confidence. As a philosopher and a logician it's hard to deal with him. When he became one of Newman's supporters, he brought great weight with him, but he became a very unaccommodating and unmanageable member of the crew.

'As far as wit is concerned,' said Mozley, 'Ward's always much too sharp for me. I always have a good answer ready for him – half an hour too late! Actually though, he's a good man and I've heard him preach some fine sermons. Despite his joviality, he's never coarse or profane – though I grant he's sometimes misunderstood by those who fail to appreciate his humour.'

We had now reached Balliol and I was eager to meet the man whom Mozley had described so vividly. Mozley's knock at the door of Ward's suite of rooms was met with a booming 'Come!' which I should think was heard half-way across the quad.

Ward's sitting-room was untidy and not very well furnished. Several tables were covered with books, pamphlets, papers, tea-things and writing materials. He was, I should say, about five feet nine in height, rather handsome though seriously overweight. His clothes were as untidy as his room. He broke into a cheerful smile when introduced to me.

'Sorry about the mess,' he said to me. 'Every so often I try to tidy up and send my loose books and papers to the binders. But they can't cope and send it all back bound up together with no regard to the subjects and labelled "Sermons, Operas, etc"! What good's that to me?'

'The labels are symbolic of you, Ward, surely!' said Mozley.

'That's what they all say,' Ward responded, then changed the subject. 'I see Arnold's launched another of his attacks on the movement. I hardly ever agree with Arnold these days,' he continued, 'but there are still things about him which I do like.'

'What things?' asked Mozley.

'Well, his hatred of worldliness, for one thing,' said Ward.

'I can't believe *you* hate worldliness,' Mozley interrupted.

Ward laughed and winked in my direction. 'I may not always achieve otherworldliness, m'self, but I admire it in others. That's why I love your brother-in-law,' he said, looking back at Mozley. 'What's more I like the reality I find in Arnold's treatment of Scripture. I like his keen sense of the "greatness of the moral idea". At Rugby, he's teaching his pupils to take a stand against worldliness; this is good, because, while the flesh and the devil are open enemies, the world's a false friend.'

'Mr Steer is interested in our attitude to "X",' Mozley said. I discovered that the leaders of the Oxford Movement hardly ever used the word 'Evangelical' in conversation among themselves. Instead, Evangelicals were known as "X", and high churchmen, or the high and dry, were known as "Y". Apparently this practice began because Newman felt that the word 'Evangelical' was a good one, referring to a fine biblical strand of truth and he didn't want to use it to refer to a party within the Church. In reply, Ward didn't seem to want to drop his references to Thomas Arnold, the famous headmaster of Rugby and recently appointed Regius Professor of History at Oxford.

'Well I'm at one with Arnold in our common opposition to one aspect of Evangelical religion. Arnold gives his pupils systematic lessons in self-improvement and the need *to struggle* against the lower tendencies of our natures. This is in marked contrast to the element of fatalism which the Evangelical party has inherited from Luther.

'The consequences in practice of the Lutheran principle of justification by faith alone fill me with horror: I see it as the destruction of the whole idea of the virtue of self-conquest. I doubt whether the principle is often fully acted on in practice – but when it is, it involves a fatal total passivity: a surrender to the Spirit or the flesh – whichever has the upper hand.

'I'm a firm believer in the ethical principle which involves an uncompromising stand against worldliness. The ethical principle loves holiness. I love the idea of glorifying God in our daily actions. We need to encourage people to pay constant attention to moral discipline and self-improvement. All this is teaching which commends itself to the conscience and the spiritual nature.'

'Where do you differ from Arnold?' I asked.

'Well, we don't agree on the interpretation of Scripture,' Ward replied. 'Arnold believes in free enquiry. But I think it would take five times the length of a man's natural life to qualify a person endowed with extraordinary genius to have some faint notion on which side of a disputed issue truth lay. What we need is some higher and more direct principle than "free enquiry" and "private judgment".

'I have this in particular in common with Newman: I recognise conscience and not the intellect as the supreme guide in religious enquiry. Conscience is our true primary informant. Conscience is directly in touch with a person's moral nature and with the first principles which that nature implies. I see Church authority as the external embodiment of conscience: the Church completes and defines, both in religious knowledge and moral precept, what conscience traces faintly and imperfectly. Conscience becomes sensitive to a higher and truer religious system in proportion as its commands are obeyed.

'Thomas Carlyle has written that "True guidance in return for loving obedience, did he but know it, is man's prime need". Now, the great thing which attracts me to a religious teacher is his personal sanctity. Our moral faculty isn't left to its unaided powers. One of the earliest lessons it teaches us is the perception of superior goodness, and the duty of putting an ardent and loving trust in the demands of that goodness. I believe that holy men are the great fountains from which moral and religious truth flows into the world. If a revelation is given, they're the authorised interpreters of it; they discriminate between the various scattered traditions which are afloat in the current of human speculation.

'Obedience must come first; knowledge afterwards. Jesus made it clear that it's by being pure in heart that we see God, not by seeing God that we become pure in heart. I see obedience as the very air in which religious faith lives; without obedience, faith languishes and dies. The man who learns truth from argument or mere trust in men may lose it again by argument or by trust in men; but the man who learns it by obedience can lose it only by disobedience.

'Like Newman, I was attracted by Hurrell Froude's vivid appreciation of the idea of sanctity, its possibility and its heights. I liked Froude's picture of the medieval Church as an absolute, independent spiritual authority, direct, uncompromising, explicit in its decrees, in contrast with the uncertain voice of the English Church. Instead of all the tensions of the English Church unsatisfactorily guided by texts of uncertain significance, Scripture was interpreted by the medieval Church with the aid of constant tradition and the Church's divine illumination.

'In Church history, the stand for moral goodness against vice and worldliness has been seen in the highest and most ideal types of sanctity. The personal struggle of the ordinary

38

Christian against his evil inclinations has been systematised and brought to perfection in Catholic ascetic works. The medieval Church never minimised the idea of the supernatural world.

'Evangelicals and, to some extent, those who have followed in Arnold's liberal tradition, are afraid of full gospel precepts like the words of Jesus "Be perfect, as your heavenly Father is perfect" (Matt. 5:48). Among them, Christianity is watered down to what seems more practicable for the average Christian than Christ's own teachings.'

I felt increasingly agitated. Ward was challenging some of my most fundamental beliefs, though I welcomed his emphasis on obedience. I couldn't find the words adequately to express so many conflicting thoughts.

'I've always looked back with pride to the Reformation and admired the Protestant tradition,' I said.

'Well, in that you're a typical Englishman,' Ward replied, smiling. 'And, of course, under Protestant systems, there are thousands of keen-minded and ardent people. But if they've good principles they're often cruelly oppressed through their lives with the consciousness that they have deep feelings which lack adequate objects to rest on. Sometimes they're tempted into the excesses of religious enthusiasm. But they haven't been overlooked by God in His gospel. They needn't go out of the routine of daily life in search of the marvellous and supernatural: it may be that they have plain duties to perform which confine them to a humdrum existence – then let them only ponder and meditate on the mysteries which surround them in it. In the plain homey circle of common duties, their heart is not less the scene of combat between good and evil spirits than it would be in the widest and most daring ventures. They're not less a spectacle to angels. They're not less by every small act of self-denial or self-indulgence acting for good or for evil on the fortunes of the universal Church.

'In the minutiae of our lives, we can carry on a watchful and incessant contest with our old nature; the devotional books of the medieval Church instilled into their readers, and those who couldn't read but were influenced by them, a careful and systematic self-examination.

'It's true that Arnold advocates a system of self-improvement which is a distinct improvement on the Evangelical notion of passive surrender to spiritual or unspiritual influence, but I'm convinced that the way of Catholic asceticism is better: it's more systematic and thorough.

'I believe that careful and individual moral discipline is the only possible basis on which Christian faith and practice can be reared. I think that the English Church today entirely neglects the duty of this sort of moral discipline. The result is that the standard of saintliness and the average level of Christian attainment is miserably low.'

As I sat and looked at Ward, he now seemed not just overweight, but immensely fat, and this somewhat reduced the impact of what he was saying about moral discipline and saintliness. Mozley told me later that evening that Ward had been known to break chairs in the Balliol common room, not just by sitting on them but by leaning on them while totally absorbed in an argument.

'The one ultimate aim presupposed in all real religion,' Ward continued, 'is personal sanctification and salvation. The Church's voice should be as the voice of God heard amid the din of this restless and sinful world, guiding us in perplexities, soothing us in distresses, strengthening us in temptations, alarming the careless and worldly, cheering the contrite and humble heart. What's the practical work looked for on the part of the Church with this aim? To put it another way: what are the conditions for sanctification and salvation?'

Mozley and I assumed this was a rhetorical question. Apparently we were right because Ward quickly resumed his discourse with enthusiasm.

'Two things are needed,' he said. 'Faith and obedience to God's will. Now I believe that in their fullest sense, these two things are intimately connected – spiritual vision depends

40

on obedience, and obedience presupposes the recognition of God's voice in the conscience.

'In my view the Protestant principle of intellectual enquiry gives no sufficient assurance of any religious truth – not even of the existence of God. I have as many reservations about the emotionalism and subjectivity of Evangelical Protestantism as I do about the liberalism of Arnold.

'I attach enormous importance to the sense of duty – what the philosopher Kant calls the only good thing in itself – the "good will" which obeys the sense of duty, the categorical imperative "thou shalt" in the human conscience: these things are as distinct from emotion as they are from merely intellectual faculties.

'Conscience may not tell us much at first, but it's a faculty which affords us a glimpse of something objective, infinitely higher in kind than the material things around us. An earnest man will set about seeing if he can cultivate the faculty of conscience and develop the glimpse into something fuller and clearer.

'True faith involves regarding any religious system with which one is brought into contact in the spirit of a learner; true faith anticipates that the religious system will have much to teach and realises that what is true in that system will take possession of the purified soul. What is false will fall away from its own inherent rottenness in proportion as the spiritual vision becomes clearer. Now, how is this purifying of the spiritual vision, this increase of the seeing power of conscience, to be gained? I answer: by obedience to God's will.'

'Disciples of Luther,' I said, 'would answer that it's by faith alone.'

'Indeed,' replied Ward. 'Luther's doctrine of justification, and the many shadows and more or less perfect reflections of it to be found in low church Protestantism, are based on private assurance and feeling. The doctrine has no direct reference to the will's efforts to conform itself to an external standard, and this defect extends to the whole Evangelical

41

view of religious belief. The individual *feels* justified and assured of salvation by faith in Christ, the Redeemer. There's little or no emphasis on a voluntary act of submission to a power outside the believer. They insist on the utter worthlessness of all works before justification, and that works after justification are the results of the Spirit within the soul.

'Moral effort in rendering the soul fit for grace, in submitting to God's will, in conforming to grace when it's given, plays no part in the Evangelical system. Election and damnation are totally arbitrary. The believer's subjective assurance results from no objective law, offers no test whereby fancy can be distinguished from spiritual perception, but begins and ends in itself.

'Luther's doctrine, as understood by his followers today, denies the first principle of morality: the principle that the struggle to do right and obedience to conscience are the springs of true moral and religious life. It has opened the door to a religion of feelings rather than of duties, and to the fanatical excesses of religious excitement. It's in direct contradiction to natural religion, which has its very foundation in the "sense of law".'

'What do you mean by "natural religion"?' I asked.

'Glad you stopped me,' Ward replied. 'Natural religion is something that Bishop Butler has written about extensively. Taking the second word, first: by religion I mean the knowledge of God, of His will, and our duties towards Him. By "natural religion" we mean that there are three main channels which nature furnishes for our acquiring this knowledge, that is our own minds (including the conscience), the voice of mankind, and the course of the world, that is, of human life and human affairs. Bishop Butler told us that Christianity, or revealed religion, is a republication of natural religion. It instructs mankind in the moral system of the world: that it is the work of an infinitely perfect Being, and under His government; that virtue is His law; and that He will finally judge the world in righteousness in a future state. But of course the idea of natural religion is far older than Butler. It was concisely stated by the Apostle Paul when he wrote, "For since the creation of the world God's invisible qualities – His eternal power and divine nature – have been clearly seen, being understood from what has been made, so that men are without excuse" (Rom. 1:20). Conscience teaches us not only that God is, but what He is; it provides for the mind a real image of Him, as a medium of worship; it gives us a rule of right and wrong and a code of moral duties.

'For many Evangelicals,' Ward continued, 'a man is acceptable, not because he conforms to the law, but because a capricious power chose him; he knows that he's acceptable, not by comparing his will to the law, but because his feelings are especially moved. In proportion as such views gain footing, agnostics are only too well warranted in identifying religion with excited emotion, and denying its claims as the guardian of moral law which it directly contradicts.

'I see the intellectual basis of Protestantism as flawed; and its ethical superstructure is no better. It exalts feeling at the expense of duty, and allows the arbitrary will of God to supersede or oppose morality itself.'

'That's a pretty damning indictment of the whole religious world in which I grew up, and which included in it some delightful, godly and devout people,' I said.

'When I say this,' Ward replied, 'I always make it clear that I'm not making accusations against individual Evangelicals, whose personal piety is often superior to their principles. I'm simply taking a view of the principles as such, that is, of free enquiry and justification by faith. I say that the inevitable tendency of these views as they become fully realised is to be subversive of true religion.

'In asserting the principle of obedience to conscience as the guide to more light, I'm insisting on the very points which Lutheranism either denies or ignores: first, the intrinsic worth of moral effort; second, the necessity, as I see it, that revealed religion should have its basis in natural religion and should develop and not contradict it; and third, the moral light which

43

comes – not from attending to subjective feelings – but from conformity to objective duty.

'Those men whose obedience has been more complete than our own, will have fuller insight into religious truth than ourselves, and will be our natural teachers.'

As a biographer, I welcomed the idea that godly men and women have much to teach us.

'What can we learn from these holy people?' I asked.

'If you study the endlessly various specimens of the saintly character,' Ward replied, 'you'll more and more clearly discern in each one of those individuals – however much they vary from one another in temperament, the time when they lived, their rank, their education, sex, age – a certain inward character, surprisingly similar to that of all the rest. Their characters demonstrate a certain complete and singular fulfilment of the gospel gift and the wonderful potential of human nature, so infinitely beyond anything which could be imagined before Christ came. In this way, we come to understand the perfect law of God.

'Above all, the lives of the saints are, as it were, spiritual ladders by which we rise into a continually fuller appreciation of Christ, Who is the one full embodiment of the law of God.

'The saints in every age are the great external witnesses of Christianity, the great visible notes of the Church. They bear witness in their own person, a far surer witness than could be borne by any external sign or proof, to the depth, reality, effectiveness of Christian doctrine. At the same time, the same holy men, not by means of formal calculation, but by the spontaneous impulse of the Holy Spirit within them, are the great originators of that infinite variety of external shapes which the one ancient truth assumes in every successive period, that it may meet the special needs of that period.'

7 Tasks for the Church

'A Church which is always on the look-out for the conversion of souls,' said Ward, 'will take advantage of those moments when an impulse towards good is felt by someone who has previously led a worldly or openly immoral life. This may be a result of a reverse in business affairs, or sickness, or sorrow or from temporary religious feelings. A watchful Church will, as it were, "fall on the neck" of someone like this and "kiss him"; she will endeavour to place religion before him in as attractive a light as possible.

'The person concerned will then face the wearisome and grievous task of retracing his steps and disentangling himself under God's grace from the miserable slavery to sinful habits. During this proccess, some wisely and religiously constituted system of observance must always be at hand to fan the embers of piety into a steady glow; the objective will be to obtain possession of the individual, as it were, to secure him from the world before it has had time to reassert its dominion, to bring before him religious truths and sanctions and impress them on his whole nature, to strengthen and protect him in holy seclusion till he may be able to go out into the world without imminent danger of falling away again from a narrow path.

'An object still dearer to the Church's heart even than comforting and restraining the penitent will be to guide those aright who have never wholly withdrawn themselves from under the Lord's light yoke. The caring Church will want to relieve their perplexities, point out their duties, direct their obedience, show them their spiritual dangers, guide their potential acts, and mould their habits after the Christian model.'

'You make the Church sound like a rather oppressive regime!' I observed.

'Well, the Church must do all this,' said Ward, 'without cramping or fettering, while she directs the free and natural development of the Christian's character, and without inter-fering with that endless diversity of opinion which must always exist on the application of true principles in each particular case. God intends there to be diversity within the Church – that's the way He works His purposes. So the Church must never substitute arbitrary ecclesiastical discipline for well regulated individual responsibility.

'An even more important function of the Church I may summarise as the "training-up of saints" – diligently tending those who, whether in reward for a consistently holy walk, or by the free working of God's grace, have aspirations within them that tend to a high and noble strictness of life, and who thirst for a far more entire self-denial and devotion to God's will than that for which the ordinary walks of life afford sufficient scope.

'The Church needs to place before Christians such as these the opportunity of consecrating wholly to God their ardent and enthusiastic feelings; in this way God will raise up for our needs, and to do His work among us, intrepid, ardent, enthusiastic, humble, holy, heavenly-minded men and women.

'And so the Church witnesses in the midst of us the great principles of morality, and is bound to assist her children in applying them to their particular circumstances, in knowing what is and isn't sin. In order to do this, the Church needs a recognised body of moral theology which will assist her in the task of implanting maxims of conduct and instilling practices of piety. But in addition, she must possess a certain number of people who are experts in the noble science of mystical theology. The best theology is never purely academic: there's a close connection between the highest attainable holiness in conduct and the knowledge of pure doctrine.

'We can think of the *duty* of a Christian (as distinct from his gifts and privileges) according to the well-known division between faith and obedience.

'Taking faith first, which includes knowledge of the great Christian doctrines: Christian precept and Christian doctrine are the two great external facts which essentially claim the Christian's attention and allegiance. And in a very remarkable manner they react on and correspond to one another.

'Pure doctrine requires for its reception a purified heart; a purified heart requires for its support and progress in holiness pure doctrine. In no other way than by the habit of strict and anxious conscientiousness can that faculty be acquired which alone hears God's voice where others don't hear it, or interprets His Word aright where all hear it. In no other way than by contemplation, reception and hearty approval of sound doctrine is this conscientiousness made really Christian obedience, preserved in its first fervour. This is the way to add refinement and delicacy to zeal and warmth, confident hope to godly fear, joyous exultation to deep contrition and humility.

'Without reading Scripture or knowing a word of it, you *may* be a good Christian (if you live where Christian tradition is preserved); without obeying Christ's commandments and believing in His doctrine, you *can't*. From the earliest days, the Church has acted on this principle. Any Church which doesn't have at her centre a deep dogmatic theology, exuberant with life, indomitable in energy, that Church is lackadaisical, wavering and unauthoritative in shepherding her flock.'

'Even if I accept the drift of your argument,' I interrupted, 'aren't there many people in Protestant Churches who have accepted the faith in which they have been brought up without question, have readily and happily performed the duties which have come their way, who live their lives in an attitude of faith and responsibility? Are you condemning them because you believe there are flaws in Protestant theology and practice?'

'I admit that there are many such: people who're not given to speculation and live a life of practical usefulness and devotion without realising the implications of the principles I've condemned. Some of them may maintain in their words or in their preaching principles which their conduct contradicts – I

47

accept this. And I agree that these excellent and God-fearing people will find what I am saying exaggerated, eccentric or unreal. A Church to them means little more than a body of men and women, and perhaps a collection of ordinances, which appeal to their higher nature and religious feelings.

'I accept that the Evangelical party has produced many pious men like Thomas Scott and Henry Martyn; nevertheless elements of Lutheranism and Calvinism within Evangelical Christianity contain the seeds of emotionalism in religion, and of the divorce of religion from morality which may result in the excesses of Methodist love-meetings. These excesses give a colourful justification to the cry of modern agnostics that Christianity has not been the preserver but the destroyer of the moral ideal, that salvation and not morality is its object. And so I always try to speak respectfully and charitably of individuals who follow the Evangelical faith, but plainly and distinctly of their flawed principles.

'And now,' said Ward, 'I want to say something to you which is very plain and, you will say, very severe. But first, let's have something to eat.'

8 Two fatal principles

Apparently there was no formal dinner in the college refectory that evening. Instead, one of the Balliol servants brought us supper on three trays. They were hearty suppers and Mozley managed to whisper in my ear a story of how Newman had once visited Ward unexpectedly on a fast day to find him sitting in front of a large beef steak – he claimed that he had entirely forgotten the fast!

During the meal, Ward broke off from his lecture on the shortcomings of Lutheranism and talked to Mozley about Newman's plans to move to Littlemore, three miles south of Oxford, where he had recently converted a stable block into a retreat for study and devotion. Littlemore was part of the parish of St Mary's, and Newman had himself raised the money for the building of a church there which was opened in September 1836.

Apparently Newman had just received a letter from the Bishop of Oxford asking him to deny a newspaper article that he was erecting a monastery at Littlemore. Newman had of course denied the report. He told the bishop that he had converted part of the stable block into a library and that the rest would be used by parish workers, those studying for ordination, or friends staying with him. They would all be involved in study and joint devotion. The bishop had replied that he was sure everyone would benefit from such a place (the buildings are still in use for similar purposes in the 1990s). After we had eaten, Ward resumed his discourse and I was anxious to discover what it was that he thought I would find so severe.

'There are two principles which are the chief marks of the Reformation,' Ward said. 'These are the Lutheran doctrine of justification and the principle of private judgment. By "private judgment" I mean the idea that has prevailed since the Reformation that each individual Christian has a right to interpret Scripture as he thinks right, or as he thinks he is guided by the Holy Spirit. On this principle the Bible succeeded in overthrowing the supremacy of the Church and the Pope.'

'Newman has pointed out that the principle of private judgment isn't held consistently,' Mozley said, turning to me. 'For if a staunch Protestant's daughter uses her private judgment, decides to become a Roman Catholic and takes herself off to a convent, he'll soon tell her what he thinks of her private judgment! Newman quotes the Ethiopian's reply, when Philip asked him if he understood what he read: "How can I, unless someone explains it to me?" (Acts 8:31). Newman says the Church undertakes this office.'

'Quite so,' said Ward. 'But the point is that I believe that in their abstract nature and necessary tendency the two principles of Luther's view on justification and private judgment sink below atheism itself.'

'You are saying,' I interrupted, 'that two principles which the devout people amongst whom I grew up hold dear, to say nothing of perhaps a majority of English Christians, are worse than atheism?'

'I am. I believe the principles are fatal. I've seen the principle of private judgment lead to infidelity – that is, the abandonment of faith. And I've seen a belief in the Lutheran doctrine of justification lead to the abandonment of moral law in favour of a religion of emotion. Churches accepting the Reformation teaching on justification tend to thwart the aspirations of holy men towards saintliness. I believe we should work for the restoration of the principles of faith and obedience, and for the destruction of the Lutheran spirit of self-righteousness and passivity.'

I noticed Mozley looking hard at me – obviously anxious to see how I was reacting. I was shocked, as they had predicted. At least they had been kind enough to warn me! Ward was enthusiastically attacking tenets which are widely held very dear.

'Just supposing you're right,' I spluttered, 'how should we set about working for the restoration of the principles of faith and obedience?'

'Well, for example, by the practical realisation of those Catholic doctrines which are presupposed in the Anglican Prayer-book. A good sign of real religious life in a Church is a consciousness of its shortcomings, and of its constant need of renewal. In a Church, as with an individual, self-righteousness must mean blindness; humility is the condition of spiritual life.

'I accept that in any Church there'll be a certain amount of failing and corruption – that's natural. But in the English Church there's a far deeper source of corruption on the moral side, while her intellectual position is hopelessly anomalous. The source of her moral corruption has been the adoption of the Reformation principle of private judgment, and the

Lutheran spirit. The compromise between Catholicism and Protestantism has reacted upon her moral tone; the Protestant doctrines which affirm justification by faith, the principle of private judgment, the rejection of the saints of the Church as fanatics, are all part of a certain general spirit.

'In contrast, the spirit of self-denial, beginning in humble obedience to conscience, and culminating in enthusiastic self-effacement for the love of God forms a coherent moral ideal. One part depends on another: reject the idea of the union between austerity and sanctity, and you have mortally wounded the whole of Catholic spirituality. You need the ascetic discipline to raise the moral tone and get rid of the self-satisfied Lutheran spirit.

'To me, Christianity is either a remedial religion or it's nothing. In other words, the Church needs to undertake constant, perhaps laborious, training of the will and affections in order to make God, sin, judgment and eternity realities to the human mind – prone as this has been to earthly rather than heavenly thoughts since the fall.

'Here are some of the spiritual weapons the Church needs to use: meditation to make the truths of religion realities to the imagination; constant examination of conscience so that sin isn't passed over or forgotten; occasional retreats as a fresh start after neglect; the literature of ascetic theology and the lives of saints to stimulate the service of God by example and precept; the Confessional for advice and consolation; moral theology to save priests from following their own whims and fancies and to give them the benefit in advising their penitents of the experience of the worldwide Church.

'I believe in the advantages of the confessional system – especially, for example, in making a wealthy man humble, delivering stern rebukes to him and gradually getting rid of his antichristian habits and principles.'

I reflected that by no means all the spiritual weapons advocated by Ward are complete anathema to Evangelicals at the end of the twentieth century: meditation is often recommended and sometimes practised; many follow the advice of the Evangelical writer Hallesby to take time to listen to the voice of God speaking to us through our conscience; retreats are increasingly popular; and the value of a first-rate, broadly-based, theological education for Christian leaders is well recognised.

'The spirit breathed by Luther's doctrine of justification by faith alone tends to make religion a matter of feeling rather than of duty,' Ward continued, 'of subjective and passive emotionalism rather than energetic discipline of the will. Lutheranism, at least as it's practised today by many Evangelicals, denies the truth that careful moral discipline is the necessary foundation upon which alone Christian faith can be reared.

'Actually, of course, the Lutheran doctrine isn't fully accepted by many. It's especially professed by the Evangelical party, but you find it among them side by side with the truly religious spirit which their habits of prayer and Bible study can't fail to produce. The inconsistency between the two – between the godly "fear and trembling" which they learn from Scripture and the assurance of salvation preached by Luther, between the idea of "working out their own salvation" and that of a salvation already secured by believing it to be secured – leads to a peculiar confusion in the doctrinal statements of Evangelicals, and an unreality in the use of them.

'As to the practical frame of mind of Evangelicals, I grant that they often do own to principles which are opposed to Luther's view. An Evangelical will adopt Luther's language, but not his view to the full: the result is a medley of ideas, and a divorce of phrases from their natural meaning. High-sounding terms and phrases are used, the fluent and familiar repetition of which are considered by the congregations an unfailing note of spirituality – while the absence of these terms and phrases is taken as an unfailing note of worldliness.

'Evangelicals seem generally remarkably unwilling to admit that holiness consists in unreserved submission, even in the smallest details and duties of our lives, to the will of God: they seem unconsciously to regard such a view as legalistic or Pharisaic. They regard complete independence of God's will as worldliness or carnality, but complete and abject dependence on it as superstition, legalism and "monkery".'

This was obviously an exaggeration, certainly when applied to the Evangelical world of the 1990s, but there was just enough truth in it to prevent my interrupting Ward.

'In the Catholic Church, from earliest days until now, there has been one and only one consistent pattern for the inner life of the believer. The Christian pilgrim has felt himself placed in this world in the midst of a severe and unceasing conflict, his bearing under which determines his lot hereafter; he's contending for a prize which needs all his efforts to secure; he's climbing up towards it by a severe and rugged path. Certainly he'll be saved if he's true to himself and faithful in following God's guidance, yet so arduous is the path of pilgrimage that sluggishness or self-security will be certain ruin.

'Certainly, the Christian pilgrim is gifted by God with the most ineffable and transporting blessings even on his pilgrimage, yet these are but faint foretastes of the far greater bliss in store for him when he reaches his heavenly home. Every suffering rightly endured, every exertion daringly and religiously ventured, increases the reward purchased for him by the One who "first bore His own cross", a cross infinitely heavier and more grievous than He has laid on any that follow Him.

'For this labour cheered by hope, the Evangelical system has substituted the listlessness caused by the doctrine of assurance; in the place of *sin* as the one evil to be dreaded, the great enemy to be feared, it puts the bogey of "self-righteousness" (as though there were almost as much danger in obeying too much as too little). For spiritual blessings won in the very innermost heart and soul, the Evangelical system speaks of the cold knowledge of our external and forensic pardon – they say that when I'm justified, it's "just-as-if-I'd never sinned".

For a noble and sustained triumph over the old man, it has, as it were, peevish and petulant complaints of his power.

'And so in my judgment, the Evangelical system cripples the noblest energies, stifles the loftiest aspirations, oppresses the tenderest feelings of those it has claimed as its followers. Therefore I feel it my duty to warn about its dangers and encourage its disciples to test its strange decrees in the light of Scripture, of conscience, of the voice of the Church.

'I say again that obedience to the will of God, with whatever sacrifice of self, is the one thing most needed; that sin is the one danger to be dreaded, the one evil to be avoided; that these great truths are the very foundation of that natural religion of which the Apostle Paul speaks in the second chapter of Romans.

'To the extent that this modern Evangelical system denies that obedience to God and the dread of sin are essential and necessary truths, and counts it the chief glory of the gospel that under it they are no longer truths, then I must plainly state my conviction that a religious heathen, were he really to accept the doctrine which Lutheran language conveys, so far from advancing as a person, would be the loser by exchanging fundamental truth (Rom. 1:19–20; 2:14–15) for fundamental error.

'In fact, as I've said, there has in practice been much sincerity and personal devotion among those who have embraced the Evangelical system; many times, individual conscientiousness neutralises the error of the teaching. But it's sad to think how the Evangelical system has crippled and bound the natural religious instincts of its victims, and prevented them from carrying that instinct forward to its legitimate development.

'And so we find this surprising phenomenon among Evangelicals: a moral and intellectual inconsistency which is surprising at first sight, but no longer surprising when we remember that they possess religious feelings which certainly draw them *to* Christ, but that they are also the inheritors of a tradition and unscriptural system (which they think most scriptural) which draws them *from* Him. The result is a feebleness, unshapeliness, dwarfishness of spiritual stature which people who are familiar with Catholic spirituality are disappointed to find among Protestants.

'A religious person is justified in rejecting Lutheranism on the same grounds as he would reject atheism, that is, that it's a contradiction of truths which he feels to be first principles.

'If it's true that the idea of duty is more deeply rooted in our nature even than the idea of God, then a serious result follows in the case of Lutheranism. When we speak of Lutheranism we speak of an abstract doctrine which can't, I believe, be held consistently, but which is held to an alarming extent among Evangelicals, though inconsistently.

'As Lutheranism is the embodiment of that spirit which denies that moral self-discipline is at the root of religion, so the Catholic system is, in my opinion, the embodiment of the spirit which affirms the centrality of self-discipline. In spite of the corruptions over time within the Catholic Church, that Church has preserved the ideal and the machinery which enables those who make use of it to aim at the ideal.

'The great principle which is at the root of all this, and which I think unites all men of good will, is the supremacy of conscience in the pursuit of moral and religious truth. What is needed in these days is a humble and religious carrying out of those great principles which the Reformation denied: obedience and faith.'

When it was clear that it was time for Mozley and me to take our leave of Ward, I told him that our conversation had left me confused and perplexed. This remark seemed neither to surprise Ward nor dampen his joviality, but I couldn't match his high spirits as we left. Three years later, the Oxford University authorities deprived Ward of his degree for refusing to withdraw his extreme views. Immediately after the dramatic decision in the Sheldonian Theatre, Ward called on Dr Pusey to discuss the situation and had to be rebuked for his spirit of levity and hilarity. He was quite incorrigible.

9 Luther's doctrine

As Mozley and I walked down St Aldates, over Folly Bridge, and on to Littlemore, where Newman had suggested we spend the night, Mozley asked me whether anything in particular had troubled me about what Ward had said.

'His views on justification,' I replied.

'Then we must visit Newman again tomorrow,' Mozley said. 'A few years ago he gave a well-attended and much-talked-about series of lectures on justification in the Adam de Brome chapel at St Mary's, which were subsequently published. Newman expresses his views in a less extreme form than Ward.'

At Littlemore, Newman had taken a lease on a row of tiny cottages which had recently been converted from an old block of farm buildings. There didn't seem much to support the rumour of a monastery. Some windows had been knocked into an old granary wall; Newman had converted the stable into a library. There was a sort of green veranda running along one side and Newman had planted some roses, wall-flowers and sweet briar.

An old and kindly man, though somewhat deaf, showed us to a couple of small rooms where – despite all the new and troublesome thoughts racing through my mind – I slept. As far as I remember, there were no dreams within the dream.

The next morning, Mozley and I returned to Oriel where Newman received us warmly.

'It's still not clear to me whether you and the other leaders of the Oxford Movement do or don't believe in justification by faith. Please tell me,' I asked Newman, 'because I was brought up, both in school history lessons and in my church, to regard the doctrine as one of the treasures of the Reformation. Mr Ward was scathing about it.'

Newman sighed.

'How long have you got?' he asked with a smile.

'I'm not in a hurry and I very much want to understand this,' I replied.

'The short answer to your question,' Newman began, 'is that I've no doubt that the way that Luther's disciples today understand justification is mistaken in theory and dangerous in practice.

'You'll find two main views about justification in the writings of English churchmen: first, that this great gift of our Lord's death is given to those who are moved by God's grace to claim it; and second, that it's given to those who by the same grace are moved to do their duty.

'Now these two doctrines, justification by faith and justification by obedience, aren't inconsistent with one another; and religious men often in practice hold both at once. Yet, though so compatible in themselves, it's a different matter altogether when people make one of these ways of looking at justification the fundamental principle of the gospel system, as Evangelicals usually do, and develop the implications of the doctrine to its limits. Then what seemed at first just two ways of stating the same truth turns out at one extreme to be the symbol of Romanism, and at the other to be that of extreme Protantism.

'In answering your question, I'll try to summarise what I said in my lectures. "Justification by faith only" is an erroneous and misleading catchphrase, while "justification by obedience" is a defective view of Christian doctrine. The former is beside the truth, the latter short of it. The former legitimately tends to the creed of the rigid Lutherans who opposed Melancthon; the latter to that of extreme Roman Catholic writers. That we are absolutely saved by obedience, that is by what we are, has introduced the proper merit of good works; that we are absolutely saved by faith, or by what Christ is, has introduced into some minds the notion that good works are actually prejudicial to our salvation.

'I'll outline the chief characteristics of the *Lutheran* view, and you can tell me whether this coincides with the doctrine you were brought up to believe. The point at which it

57

differs from the Anglican liturgy and Articles is clear. Our formularies speak of faith as in many ways essential to our justification but not as the instrument of originally gaining it. The special instrumentality of faith is the Lutheran tenet which results from attaching *exclusive* importance to the doctrine of justification by faith only.

'People who hold that the doctrine of justification by faith declares only one of several truths about our justification, even though they may express themselves like strict Lutherans, may really agree with the Church; but it's very different with people who hold it as covering everything there is to say about the way we are justified.

'This then is the peculiarly Lutheran, or what may be called the Continental view: that faith is the proper instrument of justification. That justification is the application of Christ's merits to the individual, or (as Evangelicals sometimes put it) the granting of a saving interest in Him, isn't denied by English divines. Moreover they will agree that His merits aren't communicated, or a saving interest secured, except through a God-given instrument.

'All parties seem to agree so far; but when we go on to ask what it is which God has made His instrument, then we meet the main subject of dispute between ourselves and the strict followers of Luther. The Church of England considers it to be the sacrament of baptism; they consider it to be faith.

'These two views needn't be, and haven't always been, opposed to one another. Baptism may be considered the instrument on God's part, faith on ours; faith may receive what baptism conveys. But if the word, instrument, is taken to mean in the strictest sense the immediate means by which the gift passes from the giver to the receiver, there can be only one instrument; and either baptism will be considered to convey it (whether conditionally or not, which is another question), or faith to seize, or, as they put it, to apprehend it – either faith will become a subordinate means, condition or qualification, or baptism a mere sign, pledge, or ratification of a gift which is really independent of it.

'Let's consider the system of doctrine arising out of the belief that faith not baptism is the instrument of justification. I'll try very hard to describe the doctrine fairly. Stop me if you don't think I'm being fair.

'Those who argue that faith not baptism is the instrument of justification argue this: that faith is the one principle which God's grace makes use of for restoring us to His favour and image. Born in sin, and the heir of misery, the soul needs an utter change of what it is by nature, both within and without, in itself and in God's sight.

'The change in God's sight is called justification, the change within us is regeneration; and faith is the one appointed means of both at once.

'Faith is awakened in us by the work of the Holy Spirit, generally co-operating with some external means such as the Bible; and embracing the news of salvation through Jesus, it thereby also appropriates it, becoming at the same time the element and guarantee of subsequent renewal. As leading the soul to rest in Christ as its own Saviour, and as the propitiation of its own sins in particular, it imparts peace to the conscience, and comfortable hope of heaven; and as being living, spiritual, and inseparable from gratitude towards Christ, it abounds in fruit – that is, good works of every kind. That's my first general summary of the Lutheran, or Evangelical, doctrine. Did you recognise it?'

'What you said sounded both fair and familiar to me,' I replied.

'Good,' said Newman. 'Now, the Thirty-nine Articles of the Church of England put the same sense upon the word justification – that is that it means a change in God's dealings with us – so I don't need to stop and consider it here. Let's think about what is meant by faith or trust – to which such great effects are ascribed.

'First, what faith isn't: it's explained that faith isn't mere belief in the being of God, nor in the historical fact that Christ has come on earth, suffered and ascended. Nor is faith the submission of the reason to mysteries, nor the sort of trust which is required for exercising the gift of miracles. Nor is faith the knowledge and acceptance of the sacred truths of the New Testament, even the atonement. It's neither the faith of Judas who healed diseases, nor of devils who "believe and tremble" (James 2:19 AV) – these kinds of faith don't deserve the name.

'Such is supposed to be justifying faith considered negatively: when you ask for a more direct account of it, you're likely to be told something like this: that it's a spiritual principle, altogether different from anything we have by nature, endued with a divine life and efficacy, and producing a radical change in the soul; or more precisely that it's a trust in Christ's merits and in them alone for salvation.'

'I'm very familiar with that language,' I said.

'According to this view,' Newman continued, 'faith is regarded as that very feeling exercised towards God which we are on the contrary warned against when directed towards anything earthly, as riches, or an arm of flesh. It consists in a firm reliance on Christ's mercy towards even the worst of sinners who come to Him – an experimental conviction that the soul needs a Saviour, and a full assurance that He can and will be such to it – a thankful acceptance of His perfect work – an exaltation and preference of Him above all things – a surrender of the whole man to Him – a submission to His will – a perception and approval of spiritual things – a feeling of the desirability of God's service – a hatred of sin – a confession of utter unworthiness – a self-abhorrence of what is past – and a resolution, in dependence on God's grace, to do better in future.

'Some sort of description like this is often given of faith – it's spoken of as love, gratitude, devotion, belief, holiness, repentance, hope, dutifulness and all other graces. However it's obvious that this description includes too much, as the former said too little. So what are we to say that justifying faith really is?

'The Lutheran divines say it's a "fiduciary apprehension of gospel mercy" – a belief, not only that Christ has died for the sins of the world, but that He has died specifically for the individual so believing, and a sense of confident trust in consequence, a claiming as one's own, with full persuasion of its efficacy, what He has done and suffered for all.

'Now, this is an intelligible account of it, certainly; but it isn't at all sufficient for the purpose, for this plain reason: that justifying faith is always supposed in the Lutheran scheme to be lively or to lead to good works, but such a "fiduciary apprehension" or confident persuasion, may exist without any fruit following to warrant it. Trusting faith isn't necessarily lively faith.

'Shall we then define the justifying faith of the Lutherans to be faith which is lively? This is a more adequate account of it, but a less intelligible one. For what is meant by lively? And what is the life of faith? What is it that makes it what it is? What is that, not on account of which it is acceptable (for we all acknowledge that Christ is the only meritorious cause of our acceptance), but what is that property in it which makes it (for Christ's sake) acceptable? What is the formal quality of justifying faith? If we can find this out we shall be able to understand what Lutherans mean when they speak of it.

'Many divines accordingly, of various schools, consider this life of faith to be love; and I must say that even strict followers of Luther sometimes speak as if this is what they mean. Thus they have always indulged in descriptions of faith as an adhering to Christ, a delighting and rejoicing in Him and giving oneself up to Him; all of which seem to be nothing more or less than properties of love. Luther, however, vehemently opposed such a doctrine, arguing that to say love made faith living was to deny the innate life and power of faith as such, and to associate another principle with it as a joint instrument in justification.

'Let's for argument's sake grant this; but, if so, the question recurs, *What* is the faith which justifies? Considering how important its office is, considering what exclusive stress is laid upon it in the Lutheran school, considering what severe protests are raised against anything but faith, whether grace or good works, being ascribed a share in our justification, considering that the knowledge of our possessing true faith is made a characteristic of the healthy state of that true faith, surely we may fairly ask at the outset what faith is; what that is, as separate from everything else, which exclusively of everything else is the instrument of so great a work. Surely it's fair to ask whither we are being led, before we consent to move a foot. Those who insist that only faith justifies, are bound to speak distinctly of faith.

'In answer to this question, Lutherans usually first of all forbid consideration of it – "We can't understand these things, just rest your eyes on Christ. Faith is defined not by its nature but by its office, not by what it is but by what it does. It's trust in Christ, and it differs from all other kinds of faith in that towards which it reaches forward and on which it rests". Thus it differs from historical faith, or intellectual knowledge, in that it is a taking Christ for our portion and (to use a familiar phrase) "closing with His offer of mercy".'

As Newman spoke to me, he smiled most of the time and sometimes his eyes lit up with a twinkle, especially when he said something controversial: it was almost as if he wanted to soften the impact of what he was saying – though this never diminished the conviction with which he spoke.

'So faith is thought of as consisting in this "fiduciary apprehension" of the merits of Christ, in a willingness opposite to the tendency of our proud nature, to be saved fully and freely with an everlasting salvation "without money and without price", without merit, or labour, or pain, or sacrifice, or works of any kind on our part.

'To put it another way, the gospel mercy is proclaimed openly and universally to all who accept it. No special state of mind is necessary for appropriating it; a person hasn't to ask himself if he's fit; his warrant for making it his is the freeness of the proclamation, "whoever wishes, let him take the free gift of the water of life" (Rev. 22:17). If a man feels his need of being justified, and desires it, he has simply to ask, he has simply to look at the great work of redemption, and it's his own in all the fullness of its benefits.

'Faith then as little lends itself to a definition as putting out the hand or receiving alms; it has as little of a permanent form or shape as running or kneeling; it's a momentary act or motion rather than a moral virtue or grace, though it's the work of the Spirit, and productive of all the virtues. It's the reaching forward of the heart towards Christ, determining and resting in the thought of Him as its limit, and thus deriving its character and its form from Him.

'Upholders of the ancient faith sometimes suggest to Lutherans that either faith is more than personal trust, and if so, that addition, whatever it is, is a joint instrument with it in our justification; or that if it's nothing more, then it's not necessarily living faith.

'They answer that to ask what it is in faith which makes it justifying, as distinct from all other kinds of faith, is the same as asking what it is on account of which faith justifies; that the discriminating mark is the same as the meritorious cause; and therefore that Christ Himself and He alone, the object of faith, is what makes the faith what it is.

'However, such a reply is evidently no real explanation of the difficulty. And when brought fairly to consider it, Evangelicals in the Lutheran tradition seem frankly to confess that it's a difficulty, and that it must be left to itself. They seem to agree that faith is in itself something more than trust, though they can't say what it is more. "What is not really faith may doubtless," they say, "appear to be faith; of course there must be false brethren in the Church; yet if any pretend to faith and trust, and don't go on to obey, then they haven't real trust. This is the proper inference, not that trust can exist without obedience."

'Although they find it difficult to explain, Lutherans say that those who are savingly converted are converted by means of this simple trust, which the self-deceived and carnal misuse, and which controversialists stumble at. So the argument is that faith, an act or motion of the mind

63

produced indeed by divine grace, but valueless, applies to the soul the merits of Him on Whom it looks, gaining at the same time His sanctifying aid and developing itself in good works. These works are the only evidence we can have of its being true or not. It justifies them not as being lively or fruitful, though this is an inseparable property of it, but as apprehending Christ, which is its essence.

'The alleged grounds of the Lutheran doctrine are twofold: Scripture, and the reason of the thing. As to *Scripture*: all those many texts which speak of the freeness of salvation are quoted on behalf of the principle that confident trust is the sole qualification for being justified. "Ask and it will be given to you; seek and you will find; knock and the door will be opened to you. For everyone who asks receives" (Matt. 7:7–8); "Come, all you who are thirsty, come to the waters" (Isa. 55:1); "whatever you ask for in prayer, believe that you have received it, and it will be yours" (Mark 11:24). No words, they say, can express more strongly the right of everyone who hears of the gift of God to make it his own; and his immediate possession of it, without any intermediate channel or instrument in gaining it, if he simply believes he has it.

'To these must be added the more distinct announcements of Paul about faith in particular: which, though they don't go so far as to teach that we are justified by faith *only*, yet speak of the connection of faith with justification in a very remarkable way. For example "and are justified freely by his grace . . . by Christ Jesus. God presented him as a sacrifice of atonement, through faith in his blood" (Rom. 3:24–25); and again, "since we have been justified through faith, we have peace with God through our Lord Jesus Christ" (Rom. 5:1); and again, "For we maintain that a man is justified by faith apart from observing the law" (Rom. 3:28) – tenets which certainly do speak of our being justified through faith in some very special sense, and without the aid of the law, and therefore (it is urged) without the aid of any instrument, condition or qualification at all, whether Christian grace or good work.

'Scripture then, by telling us to come for the gifts of grace and we shall at once receive them, is supposed to imply that they are dispensed without any intermediate channel between God and the soul; on the ground that they wouldn't be freely given if given through any of God's servants or ministers, angel or apostle, prophet or priest.

'So we come to the *reason* of the thing: other systems it seems have attempted to melt the heart and restore the corrupt nation by severity, threats, or motives of expediency; but the gospel alone has dared to trust itself to the principle of free and unconditional favour, yet with success as signal as has been the failure of all other methods; for the mere preaching of reconciliation with God, the doctrine of pardon, the command to take and enjoy the blessings of redemption, has been found to act upon the soul in a remarkable way for its conversion and renewal. For though numerous conversions have been made through the course of ages to the Christian faith without this doctrine (utter revolutions indeed in the principles and framework of society, the laws of nations, and the habits both of barbarians and educated minds) still (they say) these conversions were simply outward, as not being accompanied by an enlightened and heartfelt perception of the free grace of the gospel, and of its abolition of all rites and ordinances; and though doubtless, since this instrument has been used, many have abused it to their everlasting ruin, yet all this doesn't interfere with the blessedness of its effects, wherever it has been received by a truly penitent heart, and been used for legitimate purposes with meditation, prayer, watchfulness, godly fear, and a conscientious walk.

'Luther seems to speak as if Christ were that which makes faith justifying; for Christ being the one true justifier and faith being filled with the thought of Him, a justifying power is imparted to faith which in itself it doesn't have. On the other hand Luther's opponents argue that the thought of Christ may be possessed by those who haven't Christ, and therefore it is in no sense the form or characteristic principle of justifying faith; rather that love is the true form, the discriminating mark and moulding principle under which belief is converted into faith and made justifying.

'This doctrine, however, Luther rejects with great abhorrence, arguing that it makes our thoughts centre on ourselves, cuts off communication between earth and heaven, fixes faith on the love itself, instead of mounting up worthless, rude, and unformed, to receive substance, fashion, and acceptableness in Christ. Luther declares that faith justifies before and without love.

'It follows that faith may be said to claim the promised blessings as if it were meritorious, that is, by virtue of the intimate connection between it and Christ. Hence we may be said to be justified, not only by or through Christ (as the Thirty-nine Articles word it) but on account of faith. And in this sense faith is considered by Luther and his followers as imputed to us for righteousness; Christ really, Who is spiritually present in the faith, and not the faith itself, being our sole and true righteousness, in which our acceptance with God consists.

'This then is how I would outline the popular doctrine held by Luther's followers. He had two main reasons for insisting on it (both arising from his opposition to the Roman doctrine concerning good works): first, his wish to destroy all notions of human merit; second, to give peace and satisfaction to the troubled conscience (as Calvin later put it).'

10   The Christian and the law

'In insisting on his doctrine, however,' Newman continued, 'Luther also adopted another tenet, which in his system is the counterpart to the sole instrumentality of faith. He taught that the moral law isn't binding on the conscience of the Christian; that Christ has fulfilled it by His own obedience; that Christ is our righteousness, in the sense of His obedience being the substitute for ours in the sight of God's justice; and that faith is the instrument by which that righteousness becomes ours.

'Such a view of the gospel covenant met both the alleged evils against which it was provided. For if Christ has obeyed the law instead of us, it follows that every believer has a perfect righteousness, yet not his own; in that it isn't his own, it precludes all boasting, and in that it is perfect, it precludes all anxiety. The conscience has its burden removed, without being puffed up.'

I knew that this was a view of the Christian's relationship to the law which was widely held by Evangelicals in the late twentieth century, but by no means universally. Some leading Evangelical writers, including John Stott and the lawyer Sir Norman Anderson, had rejected it. For obvious reasons, I didn't intervene to explain this.

'Luther's followers,' Newman continued, 'argue that works have no share whatever in our justification, in spite of James affirming that they have – "You see that a person is justified by what he does and not by faith alone" (James 2:24). It's possible to rest in our works – they don't imply or remind of Christ's all-sufficiency; but we can't lean upon our faith, for in fact it has no real substance or strength of its own, nothing to support us; it but gives way and carries us back and throws us on the thought of Christ, in Whom it lives.

'Upholders of the ancient faith reply to disciples of Luther that since good works can't be done at all except through the grace of God, they are simply evidence that grace is with the doer; so that to view them as sharing in our justification tends to elate us neither more nor less than the knowledge that we are under divine influences is elating.

'Lutherans say that faith, however much insisted on, has so little in it to recommend it or to rest on, so little in it holy, precious or praiseworthy, as not to seduce us to self-congratulation, or spiritual or pharisaical exclusiveness, seeing our best doings in the Spirit are neither better nor more acceptable to God than those natural righteousnesses which Scripture calls "filthy rags" (Isa. 64:6) and an unclean thing. On the other hand, this doctrine doesn't tend, Lutherans say, to widen the way which Christ has pronounced to be narrow (Matt. 7:14); for, though faith is worthless, and therefore so safe a feeling, yet it isn't easy to acquire. The pride of man, they say, resists this way of salvation from its very easiness, and isn't subdued without much inward conflict. In proportion, however, as faith takes its place, its divine object is contemplated by the mind.

'To admit that we are under the law is, Evangelicals say, necessarily polluting our conscience with a sense of guilt; for since we all sin continually, while we subject our conscience to the law, we can as little enjoy the assurance of our salvation, as we can exercise implicit faith in the all-sufficiency of Christ's merits. Nor must it be inferred that the Christian isn't in fact fruitful in good works, but that they flow naturally from the simple trust of the believer; nor that he is at liberty to violate the law, but only that it's not a matter of conscience to him to keep it; nor that he will not labour to grow in grace, but only that he isn't more acceptable to God if he does; nor that he won't be watchful against falling away, but only that he is sure, unless his faith is weak, that he has salvation at present.'

'What do you say to those who hold this?' I asked.

'Well,' Newman replied, 'this theology differs from what I consider to be classic Christian truth as held for centuries in two main points: first, in considering that faith and not baptism is the primary instrument of justification and second, that the faith which has this gift exercises it without the exercise or even presence of love.

'I can't for a moment believe that anyone would accept the Evangelical system if they understood what it really means when they thought its implications through. People profess it because it is what is so commonly preached, and they graft it upon a frame of mind in many cases far higher and holier than it.

'The Lutheran view is based on a few texts detached from their context. When we read the Psalms, we find a great deal about seeking after righteousness and the heavenly gift of inward holiness. We find the Psalmist praying for what he knows is the substance of religion – obedience: this, for him, is the one thing necessary to be accepted by God.

'Scripture speaks of one gift which it sometimes calls renewal, sometimes justification. Our righteousness is simply a quality of our renewal and a distinction between being righteous and being holy isn't scriptural.

'Psalm 51 is an "evangelical Psalm" in the fullest sense – a prayer by David for forgiveness after he had committed adultery with Bathsheba. From it we see that we are forgiven by being or while we are renewed. In Psalm 119 we have a marvellous description of a man seeking after righteousness.

'From the prophets we learn that righteousness is the great gift of the new covenant (e.g. Jeremiah 31:33ff), and the fruit of Christ's earthly ministry. What is righteousness? It is a law in the heart.

'Jesus said that your righteousness has to exceed that of the Scribes and Pharisees: it must be inward righteousness – in substance what the Pharisees had only in pretence. In the parable He told of the sheep and the goats, we see the Son of Man sitting on His throne at the end of time. The sheep are those who have fed the hungry, given hospitality to strangers and clothed the poor; they are welcomed into the heavenly kingdom. The goats are those who refused to feed the hungry or help the poor; they are sent to eternal punishment (Matt. 25:31–46).

'If we look at Paul's writings we find that Paul says that justification is within; it's from God indeed as an origin but through our hearts and minds. Paul tells us that the Holy Spirit helps us obey the law; he speaks of the law of the Spirit of life making us free from the law of sin and death. He speaks of walking in the Spirit (Gal. 5:16). He makes it clear that the righteousness of the law isn't abolished under the gospel, isn't fulfilled by Christ only, but by Him as the first fruits of many brethren.

'Gospel righteousness is obedience to the law of God wrought in us by the Holy Spirit. The Spirit gives life and the law is written on our hearts; spiritual renovation is that which justifies us.

'At Pentecost we see the coming of the Holy Spirit to write the divine law in our hearts: that law so implanted is our justification. In this sense, justification is through the Spirit. Renovation is the real gift of the gospel and justification is implied or involved in it.

'Paul also wrote "no-one will be declared righteous in his sight by observing the law (that is by conformity to the external law); rather, through the law we become conscious of sin. But now a righteousness from God (that is the new righteousness introduced and wrought upon the heart by the Spirit), apart from the law, has been made known . . . This righteousness from God comes through faith in Jesus Christ to all who believe" (Rom. 3:20–2).

'Paul wrote, "it is by grace you have been saved, through faith – and this not from yourselves, it is the gift of God" (Eph. 2:8). It is the great gift even that of the Spirit, not of works done by your unaided strength in conformity to the natural law. The Christian is a new creation created in Christ Jesus unto good works. Works of the Spirit are good; works of the law are worthless.

'Paul writes of the life-giving and justifying nature of the new law which, unlike the external law, isn't only perfect in itself as a standard of truth but influential also; creative as well as living and powerful.

'James writes of a royal law, a law of liberty – the (new) law of God isn't a master, it is ourselves, it is our will. The fruit of the Spirit of the Lord is liberty acting from love and therefore not needing a law to force the believer. Love is the energy and representative of the Spirit in our hearts. Paul tells us about the course of sanctification: it begins in faith and finishes in love. Love is the perfection of religion and the fulfilling of the law; to fulfil the law is the summit of Evangelical blessedness.

'In Philippians 2:12, Paul writes "work out your salvation with fear and trembling." We see the genius of the (true) Evangelical system throughout Scripture. Jesus told an expert in the law who had spoken of the two greatest command-ments (Love God and love your neighbour as yourself) "Do this and you will live" (Luke 10:28).

'"Fear God and keep his commandments, for this is the whole duty of man" wrote the writer of the Book of Ecclesiastes (Eccles. 12:13); "it is those who obey the law who will be declared righteous" (Rom. 2:13); "Command them to do good, to be rich in good deeds, and to be generous and willing to share. In this way they will lay up treasure for themselves as a firm foundation for the coming age, so that they may take hold of the life that is truly life" wrote the Apostle Paul (1 Tim. 6:18–19).

'The Apostle John wrote, "God is light; in him there is no darkness at all. If we claim to have fellowship with him yet walk in the darkness, we lie and do not live by the truth. But if we walk in the light, as he is in the light, we have fellowship with one another, and the blood of Jesus, his Son, purifies us from all sin" (1 John 1:5–7).

'This is the doctrine concerning our justification which has the testimony of the Catholic Church in its favour and which I suppose all sober minds would accept at once, except for some notion that it contradicts the idea of justification by faith. I repeat, however, that it is in one respect defective; but it is at any rate what the rival doctrine isn't, a real doctrine and

71

contains an intelligible, tangible, practical view which one can take and use.

'The Reformers were determined to seduce us from the ancient faith; Luther introduced a new system contrary to that which, for example, Augustine taught. The old system said: our highest wisdom is to know and keep the law; the law is Christ; obedience is a matter of conscience. This new system says: our best deeds are sins; Augustine said: they are really pleasing to God.

'It's only fair to Luther to say that he indirectly renounced the extravagant parts of his doctrine at the end of his life.

'Now, the phrase "justification by obedience" is defective because in our natural state and by our own strength we aren't and can't be justified in this way. Everyone agrees about this: to deny it is the heresy of Pelagius.'

Perhaps Newman noticed a slight furrowing of my brow as I tried to remember Pelagius's error. He quickly came to my rescue.

'In the fifth century, Pelagius insisted that created human nature, essentially unimpaired by Adam's fall, could fulfil the will of God. But it's a different question altogether whether with the presence of God the Holy Spirit we can obey unto justification. The crucial question is: does justification in Scripture mean counting us righteous or making us righteous?

'I've no doubt that in Scripture, justification practically equals sanctification – by sanctification I mean the process of becoming holy. First, justification is "the glorious voice of the Lord" declaring us to be righteous, though it involves in fact a gift of righteousness; second, justification not only declares but precedes the gift which it declares: it is the "voice of the Lord" calling righteous what isn't righteous, till He makes it so.

'He sanctifies us gradually; but justification is a perfect act, realising at once in the sight of God what sanctification does tend towards; in it, the whole course of sanctification is anticipated, reckoned, or imputed to us in its very beginning.

'God doesn't let us remain in filthy rags of nature; the

72

justifying grace of God effects what it declares. Imputed righteousness is the coming in of actual righteousness. As God conducts His scriptural dispensations by prophecy, and anticipates nature by miracle, so He does in a parallel way infuse holiness into our hearts through justification. Justification declares pardon for past sins and makes the soul actually righteous.

'If the direct result of justification is actual righteousness, it isn't at all unnatural or strange that righteousness or renewal should be called our justification. I say this because justification renews, therefore it may fitly be called renewal.'

11   True renewal

'I hear a great deal today about renewal,' I ventured, vaguely hoping this wouldn't lead to a confusing conversation about how I had travelled back through time in a dream. My comment didn't appear to put Newman off his stroke.

'I think that justification and renewal are virtually convertible terms,' said Newman. 'God's justification doesn't merely work some change or renewal in us, it really makes us just.

'I believe, with Augustine, that our original nature isn't pure evil. We were created in the image of God. The natural man may have high thoughts and wishes and may love and do what is noble, generous, beneficient, courageous and wise; and yet the saturating effects of the fall make us unrighteous. This is the sense in which we are unrighteous or displeasing to God by nature, and in the same sense we are actually righteous and pleasing to Him via a state of grace. Not that there isn't great evil still remaining with us, but that justification coming to us in the power and "inspiration of the Spirit" so far dries up the fountain of bitterness and impurity, that we are released from God's damnation, and enabled in our better deeds to please Him.

'By grace we are gifted not with perfection but with a

principle hallowing and sweetening all that we are. As by nature, sin was sovereign in us in spite of the remains of heaven, so now grace triumphs through righteousness in spite of the remains of sin. The justified are just in the sense that their obedience has in it a gracious quality which the obedience of unregenerate man hasn't.

'Christians fulfil the law in the sense of pleasing God; and "pleasing" is a very significant word and well weighed. The presence of the Spirit is a sanctifying virtue in our hearts, making our obedience live and grow, so that it is always tending to perfect righteousness at its limits and in this sense making it a satisfying obedience, rising up, answering the kind of obedience which is due from us, that is to the nature of the claims which our Creator, Redeemer, and Sanctifier has upon us.

'This is the Apostle John's doctrine as well as Paul's. In 1 John 3:7 we read, "He who does what is right is righteous"; as if doing righteousness was that in which righteousness consists. So John is implying that our righteousness is a resemblance, and therefore a partial communication or infusion into our hearts of that superhuman righteousness of Christ, which is our true justification.

'A Christian's life is not only moral as opposed to vice and crime; not only religious as opposed to unbelief; not only renewed as opposed to the old Adam; but spiritual, loving, pleasing, acceptable, available, just, justifying. This is not of course the origins of our acceptance – that's the work of the cross. Saints not sinners are God's delight and honour.

'Another sense which has naturally led to the claim that we are justified by obedience is this: we can do nothing good of ourselves, but with God's grace we can do what is good. Grace leads to the power of co-operating with God; though justification, in the exact sense of the word, is an act external to us, it may be viewed as consisting in Evangelical obedience.

'Justification is in its fullness a great appointment of God towards an individual, beginning in His word spoken, and

74

returning back to Him through him over whom it's spoken, laden with fruit. It's a word having a work for its complement. I'm of course simplifying here: all the acts of God's mind are an incomprehensible mystery to worms such as we are.

'The historic Christian Church and the Reformers used the word justification in different senses: one party (the Protestant Reformers) consider it to be a mere acceptance; the other (Catholics) to be mainly renewal. The Protestant sense is more close upon the word, and the ancient use more living and real. When men (dealing with realities, not abstract conceptions) speak of justification, it is of a wonderful grace of God, not in the heavens, but near to them, even in their mouth and in their heart, which doesn't really exist at all unless brought into effect and manifested in renewal.

'Since we are often falling into sin and incurring God's wrath, we are ever being justified again and again by His grace. Justification is imparted to us continually all through our lives. In its beginnings, justification will consist of scarcely anything but pardon; all that we have hitherto done is sinful in its nature, and has to be pardoned, but to be renewed is a work of time. But as time goes on, and we become more and more holy, our justification will consist more in renewal, if not less in pardon. Christ, as our righteousness, fulfils the law in us as well as for us; He justifies us, not only in word, but in power.

'Christ,' said Newman, 'who is the well-beloved, all powerful Son of God, is possessed by every Christian as a Saviour in the full meaning of that title. He becomes to us righteousness, and in and after so becoming, really communicates a measure, and a continually increasing measure of what He is Himself.

'Paul bids us yield our members as instruments of righteousness unto God; he tells us we are "servants" or slaves of righteousness that "the kingdom of God is . . . righteousness, peace and joy in the Holy Spirit" (Rom. 14:17), and so on. The Old and New Testaments are full of characters who are described as just, holy and upright. Over and over again the sayings of Jesus indicate that righteousness is something expected and attainable.

'Paul says "the righteousness of the law" is "fulfilled in us" (Rom. 8:4 AV); and when he says "I can do all things through Christ which strengtheneth me" (Phil. 4:13 AV) Evangelicals suppose this means all things except fulfilling the law. Paul speaks often in his epistles of good and upright things being acceptable to God.

'Evangelicals maintain that two perfectly separate senses must be given to the word righteousness; that justification is one gift, sanctification another; that deliverance from guilt is one work of God, deliverance from sin another; that reward doesn't really mean reward, praise not really praise, availableness not really availableness, worth not really worth, acceptableness not really acceptableness; that Paul may allowably advise people to "work out your salvation" (Phil. 2:12); none but Peter may write that "baptism now saves you" (1 Pet. 3:21); none but John that "He who does what is right is righteous" (1 John 3:7); that when Paul speaks of "all faith" (1 Cor. 13:2 AV) he excludes true faith; and when James says "not by faith only" (Jas 2:24) he includes nothing else. Surely all this is very arbitrary, an attempt to subject Scripture to a previously formed system.

'The Protestant belief in justification by faith makes Scripture not a volume of instruction to which we may reverently draw near but at best a magazine of texts on behalf of our own opinions. The words of Scripture have precise meanings: Paul doesn't mean "righteous" at one time and "nominally righteous" at another.

'The adherents of the modern Evangelical system put great faith in their interpretation of Scripture. They should realise that to consult the context is a great advance towards the true interpretation of Scripture; they should consider the importance of the dominant idea in the use of a word despite diverse shades of meaning; they should learn that to get through to the spirit of the meaning (beyond the letter) we need to grasp the idea.

'These then are the two views: whether our state of justification or righteousness in God's sight consists in faith or renovation. Why is faith more acceptable than unbelief? Faith is acceptable as having a something in it which unbelief hasn't; what is that something? It must be God's grace, if God's grace acts in the soul and not merely externally as in the way of Providence.

'Neither Protestant nor Romanist ought to refuse to admit, and in admitting to agree with each other, that the presence of the Holy Spirit shed abroad in our hearts, the author both of faith and renewal, is really that which makes us righteous, and that our righteousness is the possession of that presence. The Holy Spirit is given us in order to produce renovation and justification.

'Christ said: "The Spirit gives life" (John 6:63), life being the peculiar attribute or state of the just. We have seen that, whereas justification is the application of Christ's merits to the individual, that application is the imparting of an inward gift; in other words, justification is a real and actual communication to the soul of the atonement through the work of the Spirit: I mean the living in us of God the Father and the Lord incarnate through the Holy Spirit. This is to be justified, to receive God's presence within us, and be made a temple of the Holy Spirit.

'This indwelling by the Holy Spirit has been promised as the distinguishing grace of the gospel. The divine presence vouchsafed to us is especially the presence of Christ; what is it to have His presence within us, but to be His consecrated temple? Whatever blessings in detail we ascribe to justification are ascribed in Scripture to this sacred indwelling.

'"Christ in us": this is really our justification, not faith, not holiness, not (much less) a mere imputation; but through God's mercy, the very presence of Christ.

'What is common to all Christians, as distinguished from good men under other dispensations, is that, however the latter were justified in God's inscrutable resources, Christians are justified by the communication of an inward most sacred and most mysterious gift. This is what is common to all, yet it's certain too, that over and above what all have, a still further communication of God's glory is promised to the obedient. "Blessed are the pure in heart, for they will see God" (Matt. 5:8).

'When we compare the various orders of just and acceptable beings with one another, we see that though they are all in God's favour, some may be more "pleasant", "acceptable", "righteous" than others, that is, may have more of the light of God's countenance shed on them; as a glorified saint is more acceptable than one still in the flesh. In this sense, justification does admit of increase and of degrees; and whether we say justification depends on faith or on obedience, in the same degree that faith or obedience grows, so does justification.

'Again, (and this is something I haven't yet talked about) if justification is conveyed peculiarly through the sacraments, as Holy Communion conveys a more awful presence of God than baptism, so must it be the instrument of a higher justification. On the other hand, those who are declining in their obedience, as they are quenching the light within them, so are diminishing their justification.

'If justification is the inward application of the atonement, we are provided with a sufficient definition of a sacrament for the use of our Church; we define a sacrament as "an outward sign of an inward grace". Christ has ordained two special sacraments as generally necessary to salvation – they are the only justifying rites or instruments of communicating the atonement which is the one thing necessary to us. The two sacraments of the gospel, as we may call them, are the instruments of inward life, according to the words of Jesus, and baptism is a birth, and at the Lord's Supper we eat the living bread. We can now see what the connection really is between justification and renewal.

'God's declaring us righteous renews us just as in the beginning He spake the word and the world was created.

But how does renewal follow justification? This is of course a mystery, but we may say that if the justifying word is accompanied by the spiritual entrance of Christ into the soul, justification is perfectly distinct from renewal, with which the Roman schools identify it, yet directly productive of it which strict Protestants deny.

'Protestants say that renewal is a collateral result with justification from faith; Roman Catholic writers say that it precedes justification. Rather, we say that Christ's sacred presence, which shines forth in the heart straight upon the word of justification, creates a renewal there as certainly as a light involves illumination, or fire heat.'

12 'Setting up the cross within us'

Looking around the room where Newman, Mozley and I were sitting, I noticed that Newman had hung a small portrait of his mother over the fireplace. I also saw that on top of the fireplace he had a crucifix from which he had removed the figure of Christ. Perhaps he saw me looking at this, for he began to talk engagingly about the cross of Jesus.

'Justification,' he said, 'is the setting up of the cross within us. The cross, planted by God's hands, is our safeguard from all evil. It's the fashion of the day to sever these two from one another, which God has joined: the seal and the impression, justification and renewal.

'You hear men speak of glorying in the cross of Christ who are utter strangers to the notion of the cross as applied to them in water and blood, in holiness and pain. They think the cross can be theirs without being applied – without its coming near them – while they keep at a distance from it and only gaze at it. They think individuals are justified immediately by the great atonement – justified by Christ's death, and not, as Paul says, by means of His resurrection (Rom. 4:25) – justified by what they consider looking at His death. Because the bronze snake in the wilderness healed by being looked at, they consider that Christ's sacrifice saves by the mind's contemplating it. This is what they call casting themselves upon Christ – coming before Him simply and without self-trust, and being saved by faith.'

'I often hear that sort of language in the pulpit. Are you saying it isn't true?' I asked.

'Well, certainly we ought to come to Christ,' Newman replied. 'Certainly we must believe; surely we must look; but the question is in what form and manner He gives Himself to us. In fact, when He enters into us, glorious as He is Himself, pain and self-denial come with Him. Gazing on the bronze snake didn't heal; what healed was God's invisible communication of the gift of health to those who gazed.

'In the same way, justification is wholly the work of God; it comes from God to us; it's a power exerted on our souls by Him; as the healing of the Israelites was power exerted on their bodies. The gift must be brought near us; it isn't like the bronze snake, a mere external material local sign, it's a spiritual gift and may be applied to us individually.

'Christ's cross doesn't justify by being looked at but by being applied; not by being gazed at in faith but by being actually set up within us and that not by our act but by God's invisible grace. Men sit and gaze and speak of the great atonement and think this is receiving it; not more truly than kneeling to the material cross itself is this to be blessed by it. Men say that faith is an apprehending and applying; faith cannot really apply the atonement; man cannot make the Saviour of the world His own; the cross must be brought home to us, not in word, but in power, and this is the work of the Spirit. This is justification; but when imparted to the soul it draws blood, it heals, it purifies, it glorifies.

'If you read Paul's epistles you'll find that the gift of the justifying cross as certainly involves an inward crucifixion as a brand or stamp causes sharp pain, or the cure of a bodily ailment involves a severe operation. In Galatians 6:14 Paul writes, "May I never boast except in the cross of our Lord

Jesus Christ". What cross? He goes on to tell us "through which the world has been crucified to me, and I to the world" – that is the cross of Calvary, issuing and completed in its reflection on Paul's soul. An inward crucifixion accompanies justification.'

As he spoke, Newman used rapid and decisive gestures with his hands, but never vehement ones.

'This passage in Galatians is the more remarkable because Paul is alluding to certain bodily wounds and sufferings as being actually the mode, in his case, in which the cross has been applied. He says to his converts "The Jews compel you to be circumcised, but we Christians glory in another kind of circumcision, painful indeed, but more profitable. Our circumcision consists in the marks, the brands, of the Lord Jesus, which effect for us, what circumcision can but typify, which interest us in His life while interesting us in His passion." The saving cross crucifies us in saving.

'Earlier in the same epistle we read, "We know that a man is not justified by observing the law, but by faith in Jesus Christ" (Gal. 2:15–16). Is this a light and pleasant doctrine? Is justification given without pain and discomfort on our part? So freely given as to be given easily – so fully as to be lavishly? Fully and freely doubtless, yet conferring fully what man doesn't take freely.

'Paul goes on to say, "I have been crucified with Christ and I no longer live, but Christ lives in me. The life I live in the body, I live by faith in the Son of God, who loved me and gave himself for me" (Gal. 2:20). O easy and indulgent doctrine to have the bloody cross reared within us, and our heart transfixed, and our arms stretched out upon it, and the sins of our nature slaughtered and cast out! Again, in the same epistle the Apostle says, "Those who belong to Christ Jesus have crucified the sinful nature with its passions and desires" (Gal. 5:24)

'It's remarkable that these passages are from the same epistle in which the Apostle peculiarly insists on justification being through faith not through the law. It's plain he never thought of faith as the direct and sole instrument of justification.

'Do you notice how similar this doctrine is with our Saviour's command to His disciples to take up their cross and follow Him? Our crosses are the lengthened shadow of the cross on Calvary.

'The following texts, all words of the Apostle Paul, illustrate the same truth: "We were therefore buried with him through baptism into death in order that, just as Christ was raised from the dead through the glory of the Father, we too may live a new life" (Rom. 6:4); "clothe yourselves with the Lord Jesus Christ, and do not think about how to gratify the desires of the sinful nature" (Rom. 13:14); "We always carry around in our body the death of Jesus, so that the life of Jesus may also be revealed in our body. For we who are alive are always being given over to death for Jesus' sake, so that his life may be revealed in our mortal body' (2 Cor. 4:10–11).

'The cross then in which Paul gloried was: not the material cross on which Christ suffered; not the actual sacrifice of the cross; but it is that sacrifice coming in power to him who has faith in it and converting body and soul into sacrifice. It is the cross, realised, present, living in him, sealing him, separating him from the world, sanctifying him, afflicting him. Thus the great Apostle clasped it to his heart, though it pierced it through like a sword; held it fast in his hands, though it cut them; reared it aloft, preached it, exulted in it. And thus we in our turn are allowed to hold it, commemorating and renewing individually by the ministry of the death and resurrection of our Lord.

'And so although the gift which justifies us is, as we have seen, something distinct from us and lodged in us, yet it involves us in its idea, in its work in us and (as it were) takes up into itself that renovation of the soul, those holy deeds and sufferings which are like a radiance streaming from it.'

13   Guaranteed by many witnesses

It's difficult to describe how fascinating I found Newman's voice and manner. His voice was lower in pitch than it had sounded from the pulpit, but it was very sweet. It had a wonderful ring of sympathy with it even when he was, to his own satisfaction at least, tearing Evangelical doctrine apart. I had never heard such a sustained attack on beliefs which I had always reckoned were soundly based on Scripture. I had to admit that he, too, grounded his beliefs in Scripture.

'You're not exactly a great admirer of the Reformation, are you?' I said, a little amused at my own understatement.

'I'm bound to say,' Newman replied, 'that the Protestant doctrine of justification seems to me a system of words without ideas, and of distinctions without arguments. Luther's words are his own, reasoned out from Scripture.

'But if I receive the doctrine of the historic Christian Church as God's truth, it's guaranteed by many witnesses who agree with one another. If I bow to some individual teacher, such as Irenaeus or Augustine, it's not from a notion of his infallibility, but on the ground of his representing the whole Church, or from a sense of the authority of men of holy and mortified lives in religious matters.

'But what binds me to yield submission to the sixteenth century, which I withhold even from the second? If I were to accept Luther's comparatively modern views I should be accepting terms and distinctions which, over and above their human origin, have no internal consistency, no external proof – no confirmation in antiquity; which, in short, simply have as their object the overthrow of Roman error.

'Surely the reverse of wrong isn't right; yet this doctrine assumes itself true because it's serviceable, proves itself scriptural by proving Romanism unscriptural; and flatters itself that it has a meaning viewed out of Romanism.

'It's a negative statement to say that justification isn't by works (and unscriptural as James specifically says it is, 2:24);

it's extravagant to say that it's by faith as the primary and sole instrument.

'There's nothing in Luther's doctrine which is precise, nothing to grapple with. When we're told for instance that faith justifies independently of its being a right and good principle – that it justifies as an instrument not as a condition – that love is its inseparable accident, yet not its external criterion – that good works are necessary, but not to be called so in controversy or popular preaching and that nothing in us constitutes our being justified – such a doctrine is, what it makes justification to be, a shadow.

'If our life is really hid with Christ in God, it follows that though we are bound to do our part and work with Him, such co-operation is the condition, not of our acceptance, or pardon, but of the continuance of that sacred presence, which is our true righteousness as an immediate origin. This distinction isn't just a matter of words, but real and practical.

'When you teach that Christ's atoning death, 1,800 years ago, and our individual baptism in our infancy so changed our state in God's sight once for all, that henceforth salvation depends on our doing our part in the covenant – that those gracious events put us indeed on a new footing, wiped out what was past, set us off fair, and are still operative in gaining for us heaven, if obedient, and present aids if believing, but that faith and obedience are the conditions of grace and glory – true all this is to the letter. Yet if nothing more is added we shall seem, in spite of whatever we say concerning the atonement and the influence of the Holy Spirit, if duly sought, to be resting a man's salvation on himself and to be making him the centre of the religious system.

'Viewed as most people will view it, this doctrine doesn't come up to the idea of the gospel as contained in Scripture, doesn't fix our thoughts on Christ in that full and direct way of which Scripture sets the pattern, as being not only the author of salvation to the whole race, but the Saviour of each, individually, through every stage of life. This I think is what they mean when they say that "Christ ought to be preached" and of the anxiety felt by some to maintain the supremacy and all-sufficiency of His righteousness.

'Many people are suspicious of those who in any sense teach that obedience justifies. They think it implies we have something in ourselves to rely upon; whereas if, as I would maintain, the presence of Christ is our true righteousness, first conveyed to us in baptism, then more sacredly and mysteriously in the eucharist, we have really no inherent righteousness at all.

'If the presence of Christ were to leave us, our renewal would go with it, and to say we are justified by renewal, only means that we are interested in Him from Whom it flows, that we dwell beneath the overshadowing power of Him Who is our justifier.

'I believe the full truth of the gospel is that the perfection which is as yet merely begun in our own nature, is anticipated, pledged, and in one sense realised within us by a present gift and that the centre on which our thoughts must be fixed, and the foundation from which our exertions must proceed, are not ourselves, but His presence, in whom "we live and move and have our being" (Acts 17:28).

'Though we need to tell men the severe side of the gospel, and dwell on their duties, and responsibilities, and the conditions on which grace is given, yet this is but one side; and when it is exclusively presented to Christians, as it is in the extreme Roman Catholic school, people are right to complain that it's cold and narrow and unlike "the freeness and fullness of the gospel".'

14 Why Jesus rose

'Christ's resurrection,' said Newman, 'is the source of our justification. In Romans 4:25 we read, "He was . . . raised to life for our justification."

'Whatever is done to us by the Spirit, is done within us; whatever is done in the Church since Christ's ascension, is done by the Spirit; from which it follows that our justification, being a present work, is an inward work, and a work of the Spirit. This is supported by the text in Romans, for in saying that Christ *rose again* for our justification it implies that justification is through that second Comforter whom that resurrection brought down from heaven.

'Christ atones by the offering of Himself on the cross; and He justifies by the mission of His Spirit. His atonement is His putting away the wrath of God for our sins. In order to do this, He took flesh: He accomplished it in His own person, by His crucifixion and death. Justification is the application of His precious atonement to this person or that person, and this He accomplishes by His Spirit. For He ceased to act towards us by His own hand from the day of His ascension; He sent His Spirit to take His place – "I will not leave you as orphans". He says "I will come to you" – "I will ask the Father, and He will give you another Counsellor to be with you for ever" (John 14:16,18).

'Whatever then is done in the Christian Church is done by the Spirit. The Holy Spirit realises and completes the redemption which Christ has wrought in essence and virtue. If the justification then of a sinner is a continual work, a work under the New Covenant, it must be the Spirit's work and not Christ's. The atonement for sin took place during His mission, and He was the sole agent; the application of that atonement takes place during the mission of His Spirit, who is the sole agent in it.

'There was but one atonement; there are ten thousand justifications. What was offered "under Pontius Pilate" in flesh and blood, is partaken again and again in the power and the virtue of the Spirit. God the Son atoned; God the Holy Spirit justifies. Further, it would appear as if the giving to the Father was in fact the same thing as His coming to us spiritually. His rising was the necessary condition of His applying to His elect the virtue of that atonement which His dying wrought for all men.

'Christ died in the flesh; He rose again "through the Spirit of holiness" (Rom. 1:4) which, when risen, He also sent out from Him, dispensing to others that life whereby He rose Himself. He atoned, I repeat, in His own person; He justifies through His Spirit.

'The divine life which raised Jesus flowed over and makes possible our rising again from sin and condemnation. It wrought a change in His sacred manhood which became spiritual without His ceasing to be a man, and was in a wonderful way imparted to us as a new, creating, transforming power in our hearts.

'This is what Paul means when he talks about the "incomparably great power for us who believe. That power . . . of his mighty strength, which he exerted in Christ when he raised him from the dead" (Eph. 1:19–20); and the blessedness of knowing Him and "the power of his resurrection" (Phil. 3:10) and again our being made "alive with Christ", and raised up "and seated with him in the heavenly realms in Christ Jesus" (Eph. 2:5,6).

'Now if justification, or the imparting of righteousness, is a work of the Holy Spirit, a spiritual gift or presence in the heart, it is plain that faith, and faith alone, can discern it and prepare the mind for it, as the Spirit alone can give it. Thus faith is a mysterious means of gaining gifts from God, which cannot otherwise be gained; if it was necessary for our justification that Christ should become a quickening Spirit and so be invisible; therefore it was necessary for the same in God's providence that we should believe.

'As the Spirit is the only justifier, so faith is the only recipient of justification. The eye sees what is material; the mind alone can embrace what is spiritual. So I repeat that this is our justification, our ascent through Christ to God, our God's descent through Christ to us; we may call it either of the two. And this is our true righteousness – not the mere name of righteousness, not only forgiveness, or favour as an act of God's mind, not only sanctification within: it implies the one, it involves the other, it's the indwelling of our glorified Lord. This is the one great gift of God purchased by the atonement, which is light instead of darkness and the shadow of death, power instead of weakness, bondage and suffering, Spirit instead of flesh, which is the token of our acceptance with God, the propitiation of our sins in His sight, and the seed and element of renovation.

'What I have said will throw light on an important feature of the apostles' preaching: they insist on our Lord's resurrection as if it were the main doctrine of the gospel; but why so, and not on His divinity or the atonement? Many good reasons could be given for this; as for instance, that the resurrection was the great miracle and evidence of the divinity of the religion; or that it's the pledge of our resurrection; or that His divinity and atonement was too sacred a doctrine to preach to the world. But if the resurrection is the means by which the atonement is applied to us, if it's our justification, if in it are conveyed all the gifts of the grace and glory which Christ has purchased for us, if it's the commencement of His giving Himself to us for a spiritual sustenance, of His feeding us with that bread which has already been perfected on the cross and is now a medicine of immortality, it's the doctrine which is most immediate to us, in which Christ most closely approaches us, from which we gain life, and out of which issues our hopes and duties.

'Christ is God from everlasting; He became man under Caesar Augustus, He was an atonement for the world on the cross, but He became a Saviour on His resurrection. He was then "exalted to be a prince and a Saviour"; to come to us in the power of the Spirit, as God, as man, and as atoning sacrifice.'

15   The faith which justifies

It had always seemed to me, before I had this remarkable dream, that the explanation of the apparent contradiction between Paul ('we are justified by faith') and James ('we are justified by works') must lie somewhere in the definition of faith. So I decided to pop a question to Newman about this while I had the chance.

'What sort of faith justifies?' I asked. 'What's the nature of justifying faith?'

'Well,' replied Newman, 'Hebrews 11:1 says, "faith is being sure of what we hope for and certain of what we do not see." The text is the nearest thing in Scripture to a formal definition of faith. Our Church has nowhere defined faith. Religious faith is "the substance" or the realising of what as yet isn't seen, but only "hoped for"; it's making present what is future.

'Again, faith is "the evidence" of what isn't seen, that is the ground or medium of proof, on or through which it's accepted as really existing. In the world of nature we find out about things around us by sight; and things which are to be by reason; but faith is our informant about things future which we don't see, and things future which we can't forecast.

'As sight contemplates form and colour, and reason the processes of argument, so faith rests on the divine word as the token and criterion of truth. And as the mind trusts to sense and reason, or on natural instinct, which it freely uses prior to experience, so in a parallel way, a moral instinct, independent of experience, is its impelling and assuring principle in assenting to revelation as divine.

'By faith then is meant the mind's perception of heavenly things, arising from an instinctive trust in the divinity or truth of the external word, informing it concerning them. Whether it acts upon that knowledge so obtained, depends upon something beyond – a particular moral state in a given case.

'Faith, then, isn't a virtue or grace in its abstract nature; else evil spirits (see Jas 2:19) couldn't possess it. It lives only under circumstances or in the particular case: Abraham's faith involved self-denial, Mary's (the mother of Jesus) implied love and hope. Faith is but an instrument, acceptable when its possessor is acceptable. And in this respect it differs from most other graces; that it's only an excellence when it's grafted into a heart that has grace.

'The devils can't have love, humility, meekness, purity, or compassion – they have faith. When, however, faith is so grafted, then it makes progress, and the last becomes the first. Then it becomes the instrument of securing that favour which more properly attaches to the soul exercising it; as the eye is said to see, whereas it's the organ of the mind.

'But though faith, considered by itself, isn't a grace, it must be borne in mind that it never does exist by itself; it always exists in this person or that, and, as exercised by the one or the other, it must be either a grace or not. Faith in the abstract is a mere idea of our minds. The devils believe, and Christians believe; we may compare the two; and observe that the outline of the faith in each is the same; they both realise the unseen and future resting on God's Word. But an outline never exists by itself; it always exists in a certain body or substance.

'It would seem then that Luther's doctrine, now so popular, that justifying faith is trust, comes first, justifies by itself, and then gives birth to all graces, isn't tenable; such a faith cannot be, and if it could, wouldn't justify. Mere trust as little gives birth to other graces as mere faith. It's common indeed to say that trust in the mercy of God in Christ ensures all other graces, from the fertilising effect of the news of that mercy in the heart. But surely that blessed news has no such effect unless the heart is *softened* to receive it; that softening is necessary to justification, and by whatever name it's called, spiritual-mindedness, or love, or renewal, it's something more than trust.

'Something more than trust is involved in justifying faith, or it's the trust of a renewed or loving heart. But after all it's an abuse of terms to define faith to be trust, unless one might call the devil's faith despair. Faith is neither trust nor despair, but faith; though it takes the colour of trust or of despair, according to the mind into which it is received.

'Justifying faith, then, may be considered from two main points of view; either as it is in itself, or as it exists in fact in those who are under grace. From the former point of view it's not even a moral virtue; but when illuminated by love, and ennobled by the Spirit, it's used as a name for all graces together, as having them all as its attendants and comparisons.

'I believe that Evangelicals have adopted a false position. Their idea of faith is a mere theory, neither true in philosophy nor in fact; and hence it follows that their whole theology is shadowy and unreal. I don't say that there's no such thing as a trusting in Christ's mercy for salvation, and a comfort resulting from it. This would be resisting what we may witness daily, and what it's our duty to exercise. Bad and good feel it. What's so unreal is to say that it's necessarily a holy feeling, that it can be felt by none but the earnest, that a mere trust, without anything else, without obedience, love, self-denial, consistent conduct, conscientiousness – that this mere trust in Christ's mercy, existing in a mind which has yet no other religious feeling, will necessarily renew the soul and lead to good works. This is the mere baseless and extravagant theory I speak of.'

I thought about this. Newman had had a lot to say. I would have been glad to have intervened with a remark which blew a hole in his self-confident demolition of a central plank of Evangelical theology. But I could think of nothing to say. One reason for my silence was that I vividly recalled a very low period in my life when it had seemed that everything about me was crumbling and I had thought, 'I've nothing left now but my faith. I must trust.' But then, in the depths of my despair, I had thought, 'But what is faith? What is trust? Where will it get me and how can it help me now?' Was it, I wondered, as Newman resumed his discourse, because my whole theology was shadowy and unreal? I wasn't sure – all I knew was that for the moment I couldn't spot any loophole in Newman's view of faith: and it did seem *practical*.

'Men may be conscious they trust,' Newman was saying, 'they may be conscious they gain comfort from trusting; they can't be conscious that such a trust is practical; they can't be conscious that it changes the heart. That it raises present emotions they may be conscious, that it's such as permanently to impress their inner man they can't know, unless they're prophets. Viewed in its theological aspect, in which it's now before us, it will be found to give a character of vagueness to the whole system built upon it.

'Hence, not surprisingly, it's a source of never-ending disputes between people who seem to agree, yet go away and act differently, and still wonder why they differ. I describe faith, and another describes it, and perhaps we may even use the same terms, and yet agree in nothing else.

'Faith isn't justifying unless informed and animated by love; isolated or bare faith being impossible in a Christian or in anyone else, existing only in our conceptions, and not being a grace or virtue when so conceived. Paul says, "if I have a faith that can move mountains, but have not love, I am nothing" (1 Cor. 13:2). And James, after warning his readers against having the faith of Christ "with respect of persons" that is, by showing favouritism in an unloving spirit, as the context shows, proceeds to say, that "by works was faith made perfect" and that "without works" faith is as "dead" as the body without a spirit (Jas. 2 AV).'

At last, I thought of another intervention.

'But if all you say is true,' I interrupted, 'how is it that faith has that very special role which the Bible gives it? If it isn't even a virtue itself, but indebted for all its excellence to other qualities, why do the Bible writers devote whole chapters to it?'

'The gospel,' Newman replied, 'is especially the system of faith and "the law of faith"; its obedience is the "obedience of faith"; its justification is "by faith", and it's a "power of

God unto salvation to everyone that believes", as contrasted with all religious systems which have gone before and come after, even those in which God has spoken. Faith, which in the natural man has manifested itself in the fearful energy of superstition and fanaticism, is in the gospel grafted on the love of God, and made to mould the heart of man into His image.

'The apostles didn't rest their cause on argument; they didn't appeal to eloquence, wisdom or reputation; nor did they make miracles necessary to the enforcement of their claims. The apostles came as commissioned from Him, and declared that mankind was a sinful and outcast race – that sin was a misery – that the world was a snare – that life was a shadow – that God was everlasting – that His law was holy and true, and its sanctions certain and terrible – that He also was all-merciful – and that He had appointed a mediator between Him and them, Who had removed all obstacles, and wanted to restore them, and that He had sent them to explain how. They said that mediator had come and gone, but left behind Him what was to be His representative till the end of all things, His mystical body the Church, in joining which lay the salvation of the world.'

16 Faith and works

'But I still don't understand the relationship of faith to rites and works' I persisted. 'Paul says we are justified by faith; Anglican Articles and Homilies say by faith only; James says we are justified by works. How can all these statements be true?' I asked.

'Let me tell you how I understand them,' Newman said. 'In Romans 3:28 Paul writes, "For we maintain that a man is justified by faith apart from observing the law"; in saying this, he's certainly not asserting that we're justified by faith without the deeds of the gospel. We don't contradict Paul to assert we are justified by faith with Evangelical works, unless James contradicts him also. Those who object to the doctrine of justification through good works, must first object to James's epistle, which many of them have done. On the other hand, Christian humility will lead the disciples of Paul to submit to James – they surely don't want, in condemning the Epistle of James, to resist an apostle!

'To those who judge severely of the maintenance of justification by works I say this: Why be so bent on forcing two inspired teachers into adopting contradictory doctrines? If you could prove ever so cogently that when Paul said "deeds of the law" he meant to include Christian works, you wouldn't have advanced one step towards interpreting James or impairing his authority; you would have only plunged into a more serious perplexity. If it's difficult to understand Paul insisting on faith, and James insisting on works, surely it isn't so great as to have proved that Paul excludes the very works which James includes?

'The Jews sought to be justified by works done in their own unaided strength, by the law as it was set before them in the Mosaic covenant; and Paul shows them a more excellent way. He proposes to them the law of faith, and says that a man is justified by faith without the deeds of the law; moreover, in so teaching, so far from making the law void through faith, he establishes it.

'Paul means to say this to Jews: "Throw yourselves on God's mercy, surrender yourselves to Him; the law in which you pride yourselves, holy as it is in itself, has been to you but an occasion of sin. You're in bondage; you have no real sanctity, no high aims, no inward growth, no power of pleasing God. Instead of having done anything good, you have everything to be forgiven. You must begin over again; you must begin in a new way, by faith; faith only, nothing short of faith, can help you to a justifying obedience. But faith is fully equal to enabling you to fulfil the law. Far then from invalidating the law by the doctrine of faith, I establish it."'

For a while, Newman had been looking at the floor as he

spoke. But at this point he looked up again, as if he had something particularly important to say, and looked right into my eyes.

'Justification comes *through* the sacraments; is received *by* faith; *consists* in God's inward presence; and *lives* in obedience,' he said.

This was neat, but it still didn't satisfy me. It was a minute or two before I could formulate a response.

'It doesn't follow that works done in faith don't justify, because works done without faith don't justify,' Newman continued. 'Paul urges on his brethren the one way to salvation, which, as it's Christ Himself in God's sight, so it's faith on our part. He tells them they must be justified on a new principle; new, that is, as being used under the gospel for higher purposes than before.

'If we refuse, not to modify, but even to complete one text of Scripture by another – will not adjust the second merely because we prefer an interpretation of the first which contradicts it – will not hold two doctrines at once, merely because the text that declares the one doesn't also declare the other – if we won't say with James that works justify, merely because Paul says faith justifies and works without faith don't justify – if we will demand that the whole of the gospel should be summarised in a single text – then surely we ought to hold that baptism is sufficient for salvation, because Peter says it "saves" us (1 Pet. 3:21) or hope sufficient, because Paul says "we are saved by hope" (Rom. 8:24) – or that only love is the means of forgiveness because Jesus says "her many sins have been forgiven – for she loved much" (Luke 7:47) or that faith doesn't save because James asks "Can such faith save?" (Jas. 2:14) or that keeping the commandments is the whole gospel because Paul says it has superseded circumcision (1 Cor. 7:19)?

'Nothing surely is more suitable than to explain justifying faith to be a principle of action, a characteristic of obedience, or sanctifying power, if by doing so we reconcile Paul and James and at the same time observe the very same rule of interpretation which we apply to Scripture generally.'

'But aren't Evangelicals right,' I suggested, 'to argue that under the gospel, ordinances are of little account, and that to insist on them is to bring the Church into bondage? If baptism conveys spiritual regeneration, or the apostolic succession is the warrant for the ministry, or the laying on of hands is a spiritual benefit, or consecration is required for giving and receiving the Lord's Supper, in a word, if outward signs are a necessary means of gospel grace, then surely Paul's statement doesn't hold that we are "justified by faith without the deeds of the law"?'

'I often hear this argument,' Newman replied, 'and I understand it, but it proves too much: it would prove that Christian rites should altogether be superseded as well as Jewish. For example, faith superseded circumcision; it didn't supersede baptism.'

'Surely,' I said, 'by the doctrine of faith Paul meant to magnify God's grace, to preach Christ's cross, to stipulate its all-sufficiency for pardon and renewal, and our dependence on the aid of the Holy Spirit for the will and the power to accept these blessings? If you say that sacraments are the means of justification, you obscure the free grace of the gospel. You're putting the followers of Christ into bondage.'

'I agree,' Newman replied, 'that faith exalts the grace of God; that's its office and charge; so whatever furthers this object, co-operates with the gospel doctrine of faith; whatever interferes with this object, contradicts the doctrine. Salvation by faith only is but another way of saying salvation by grace only. The gospel doctrine of faith is intended to humble man, and to remind him that nothing he can do of himself can please God; so that "by faith", means "not by works of ours". If then the sacraments obscure the doctrine of free grace, and tempt men to rely upon their own doings then they make void the doctrine of faith; if not, then they don't; they magnify God and humble man – they promote the gospel of grace.

96

'I say that the sacraments promote the object aimed at by the doctrine of faith, as fully as the Jewish ordinances counteracted it. If this is so, the doctrine of justification by sacraments is altogether consistent, or rather coincident with Paul's doctrine in the text, that we are justified apart from observing the law.

'Paul says that "by observing the law no-one will be justified" (Gal. 2:16) and James that "a person is justified by what he does and not by faith alone" (Jas. 2:24). Are these statements consistent? To condemn works without faith is surely quite consistent with condemning faith without works. James says we are justified by works, not by faith only; Paul implies by faith not by works only. Paul says that works aren't available before faith; James that they are available after faith. James speaks of works done under what he calls "the royal law", "the law of liberty" which we learn from Paul is "the law of the Spirit of life" (Rom. 8:2) for "where the Spirit of the Lord is, there is freedom" (2 Cor. 3:17), in other words the law of God as written on the heart by the Holy Spirit.

'Paul speaks of works done under the letter, James of works done under the Spirit. This is surely an important difference in the works respectively mentioned. James speaks not of mere works, but of works of faith, of good and acceptable works. I don't suppose that anyone will dispute this; then James says we are justified not by faith only but by *good* works.

'Now Paul isn't speaking at all of good works, but of works done in the flesh and of themselves "deserving God's wrath and damnation". He says "without works", he doesn't say without "good works" whereas James is speaking of them solely. Paul speaks of "works done before the grace of Christ and the inspiration of His Spirit"; James of "good works which are the fruits of faith and follow after justification". Faith surely may justify without such works as "have the nature of sin" and yet not without such as "are pleasing and acceptable to God in Christ".

'Paul never calls those works which don't justify "good works" simply "works", "works of the law", "deeds of the law", "works not in righteousness", "dead works" – what have these to do with works or the fruit of the Spirit? Note that he says, "by grace you have been saved, through faith . . . not by works, so that no-one can boast. For we are God's workmanship, created in Christ Jesus to do good works" (Eph. 2:8–10). Surely this indicates that the works which don't justify aren't good, or in other words, are works before justification. As to works after, which are good, whether they justify or not, he doesn't decide so expressly as James, the error he had to resist leading him another way. He speaks elsewhere of: abounding in every good work (2 Cor. 9:8); bearing fruit in every good work (Col.1:10); being adorned with good works (1 Tim. 2:10 AV); being well known for good deeds (1 Tim. 5:10); being rich in good deeds (1 Tim. 6:18); being thoroughly equipped for every good work (2 Tim. 3:17); being unfit for doing anything good (Titus 1:16); setting an example by doing what is good (Titus 2:7); being ready to do whatever is good (Titus 3:1); and being careful to devote oneself to doing what is good (Titus 3:8). The writer to the Hebrews uses similar expressions.

'James, though he means good works, drops the epithet, and says only works. Why doesn't Paul do the same? Why is he always careful to add the word good? Surely the reason is that he had also to do with a sort of works with which James had to do – that he applied the word *works* to those of the law, and therefore that the epithet *good* was necessary, lest deeds done in the Spirit should be confused with them.

'Paul, then, speaking of faith as justifying without works means without corrupt and counterfeit works, not without good works. And he doesn't deny what James affirms, that we are justified in good works. Such has always been the Catholic way of reconciling the two apostles and certainly without violence to the text of Paul.

'Think of faith as a *habit* of the soul: now a habit is something permanent, which affects the character.

'The writer to the Hebrews uses the same instances as James. He says, "By faith Abraham, when God tested him, offered Isaac as a sacrifice" (Heb. 11:17) and James, "Was not our ancestor Abraham considered righteous for what he did when he offered his son Isaac on the altar?" (Jas 2:21); the writer to the Hebrews says, "By faith the prostitute Rahab, because she welcomed the spies, was not killed with those who were disobedient" (Heb. 11:31); James says "In the same way, was not even Rahab the prostitute considered righteous for what she did when she gave lodging to the spies and sent them off in a different direction?" (Jas 2:25). Don't these parallels show that faith is practically identical with the works of faith, and when it justifies, it's as existing in works?

'The same doctrine is contained all through Scripture. God's mercies are again and again promised to works, sometimes of one kind, sometimes of another, though in all cases, as acts and representatives of faith. For example, in the Prophet Isaiah justification is ascribed to good works generally. He says "Though your sins are like scarlet, they shall be as white as snow" and "though they are red as crimson, they shall be like wool." Here's an Evangelical promise; why then is there nothing about justifying faith? Surely because faith is signified and is secured by other promises requiring good works. So Isaiah goes on to say: "wash and make yourselves clean. Take your evil deeds out of my sight! Stop doing wrong, learn to do right! Seek justice, encourage the oppressed. Defend the cause of the fatherless, plead the case of the widow" (Isa. 1:16–18).

'Similiarly, the Lord's word to Ezekiel about the righteous man is that, "None of the sins he has committed will be remembered against him. He has done what is just and right; he will surely live" (Ezek. 33:16).

'Zacharias and Elisabeth were both "upright in the sight of God, observing all the Lord's commandments and regulations blamelessly" (Luke 1:6). Words can't be stronger to express the justification of these holy ones – the gift not coupled with faith but with acts of obedience paid to the special and particular commandments of God.

'In the same way John says: "if we walk in the light, as he is in the light, we have fellowship with one another, *and the blood* of Jesus, his Son, purifies us from all sin" (1 John 1:7). To these may be added examples like Christ's warning to the two brothers of the consequences of becoming His disciples; His bidding us count the cost of following Him, and taking up the cross, denying ourselves and coming after Him.

'And so as works are acts of faith, so the mental act of faith is a work. Thus Jesus says to the father of a boy with an evil spirit, "Everything is possible for him who believes", and he answers "I do believe; help me overcome my unbelief!" (Mark 9:23–4).

'Paul speaks of Abraham who "did not waver through unbelief regarding the promise of God, but was strengthened in his faith and gave glory to God, being fully persuaded that God had power to do what he had promised." "That is why" he adds, "it was credited to him as righteousness" (Rom. 4:20–2).

'If you study Luther's writings you'll find that he believed faith was a work – it's his followers, highlighting slogans, who have distorted his thought.

'So, you asked about the relationship of faith to outward works and I say that, viewed as justifying, it lives in them.

'Such is faith, springing up out of the immortal seed of love, and ever budding forth in new blossoms and maturing new fruit, existing in feelings but passing into acts, into victories of whatever kind over self, being the power of the will over the whole soul for Christ's sake, constraining the reason to accept mysteries, the heart to acquiesce in suffering, the hand to work, the feet to run, the voice to bear witness, as may be.

'It seems that whereas trust on our part fitly answers or is the correlative, as it is called, to grace on God's part, sacraments are simply God's acts of grace, and good works are simply our acts of faith; so that whether we say we are justified by faith, or by works, or by sacraments, all these just mean this doctrine, that we are justified by grace, which is given through the sacraments, obtained by faith, and manifested in works.'

17   True gospel preaching

I looked again at Newman's room. Beside the door were bookcases filled with folio volumes of the early Church Fathers: Ambrose, Jerome, Augustine, Gregory, Chrysostom and Athanasius. I knew that Newman and the other leaders of the Oxford Movement had made themselves experts in the study of the Fathers and that even some Evangelicals had welcomed their tireless efforts to publish new editions of their writings. But where did all this learning get us? Had it left Newman with what Evangelicals call 'a burden for souls'? I decided to broach the subject.

'In the light of what you've told me about justification,' I asked him, 'how do you see the task of evangelism?'

'When we preach,' Newman replied, 'the one object we should put before them is "Jesus Christ is the same yesterday and today and for ever" (Heb. 13:8). True gospel preaching is to enlarge, as they can bear it, on the person, natures, attributes, offices, and work of Him who once regenerated them and is now ready to pardon; to dwell upon His recorded words and deeds on earth; to declare reverently and adoringly His mysterious greatness as the only-begotten Son, one with the Father, yet distinct from Him; eternal yet begotten; a Son, yet a Servant; and to set out His attributes and relations to us as God and man, as our Mediator, Saviour, Sanctifier and Judge.

'True preaching of the gospel is to preach Christ. But the fashion of the day has been instead to attempt to convert by insisting on conversions; to tell them to take care they look at Christ, instead of simply holding up Christ; to tell them to have faith, rather than simply to supply its object; to lead them to work up their minds instead of impressing on them the thought of Him who can savingly work in them.

'The preacher of the gospel needs to bid them to be sure that their faith is justifying, that it isn't dead, formal, self-righteous, or merely moral instead of glorifying Him, whose image fully set out, destroys deadness, formality, and self-righteousness. The preacher shouldn't rely on words, vehemence, eloquence, and the like; instead he should aim at conveying the one great idea whether in words or not.

'Let us preach Christ, and leave the effect to God. The danger of much popular preaching today is that men will feel this and that because they're told to feel it, because they think they ought to feel it, because others say they feel it themselves; it's much better that they should feel these things spontaneously, as the result of the objects presented to them.

'Let me quote from the text of an actual Evangelical sermon I read: "You may attend your church twice on Sunday, you may go on weekdays too. You may frequent the sacrament. You may say prayers in your house and alone. You may read the Psalms and lessons of the day. You may be neither given to swearing, nor drink, nor lewdness, nor extravagance. You may be a tender parent, a careful master, and what the world calls an honest man; you may be very liberal to the poor; be regarded in the world as a pattern of piety and charity, and respected as one of the best sort of people in it; and yet with all this, be the character, which 'though highly esteemed among men, an abomination in the sight of God'. For if you've never seen" (not your Saviour, but) "your desperately wicked heart been united to Christ" (by His love and grace? No but) "by faith – renounced your own righteousness to be found in Him, and received from Him newness, if you don't know experimentally what is meant by 'fellowship with the Father and His Son Jesus Christ', if your devotion hasn't been inspired 'by faith which worketh by love', if your worship hasn't been in 'spirit and truth' from a real sense of your wants, and an earnest desire and expectation of receiving from Him 'in Whom all fullness dwells', if this hasn't been your case, your devotions have been unmeaning ceremony, your book not your heart has spoken; and instead of the fervent effectual prayer of the righteous man, your babblings have been no better than the sounding brass and tinkling cymbal".'

Although today's language is somewhat different, I had to admit to myself that I had certainly heard similar sermons in my own time – though perhaps there had been a trend away from them. Newman was not slow to tell me his own view of this sort of preaching.

'Poor miserable captives, to whom such doctrine is preached as the gospel! What! Is this the liberty wherewith Christ has made us free, and wherein we stand, the home of our thoughts, the prison of our sensations, the province of self, monotonous confessions of what we are by nature, not what Christ is in us, and a resting at best not on His love towards us, but in our faith towards Him?

'This is nothing but a specious idolatry; a man taught like this doesn't simply speak of God when he prays to Him, but is observing whether he feels properly or not; doesn't believe and obey, but considers it enough to be conscious that he is, as he thinks, warm and spiritual; doesn't contemplate the grace of the blessed eucharist, the body and blood of his Saviour Christ, except as a quality of his own mind.

'You see the Church considers the doctrine of justification by faith to be only a *principle*, and the popular religion of the day takes it as a *rule of conduct*. Principles are great truths or laws which embody in them the character of a system, enable us to estimate it, and indirectly guide us in practice; but we shall be sure to get into difficulty or error if we attempt to use them as guides in matters of conduct and duty. They mean nothing, or something wide of the truth, if taken as literal directions.

'Now justification by faith only is a principle, not a rule of conduct; and the popular mistake is to view it as a rule. This is where people go wrong. They think that the way by which they must set out to practise religion is to *believe* as something independent of every other duty; as something which can exist in the mind itself, and from which all other holy exercises follow; to believe, and from then they will be justified.

'They who *are* justified, are justified by faith; but having faith isn't any more the way to be justified, than being hidden is the way to be a saint. The doctrine of justifying faith is a summary of the whole process of salvation from first to last; a sort of philosophical analysis of the gospel, a contemplation of it as a whole, rather than a practical direction.

'If it must be taken as a practical direction, and in a certain sense it may, then we mustn't call it justification through faith but justification by Christ. Thus interpreted, the rule it gives is, "go to Christ"; whereas justification through faith seems to say merely "Get faith; become spiritual; see that you're not mere moralists, mere formalists, see that you feel. If you don't feel, Christ will profit you nothing: you must have a spiritual taste; you must see yourself a sinner; you must accept, apprehend, appropriate the gift; you must understand and acknowledge that Christ is the 'pearl of great price'; you must be conscious of a change wrought in you; for the most part going through the successive stages of darkness, trouble, error, light and comfort".

'And so the poor and sorrowful soul, instead of being led at once to the source of all good is taught to make much of the conflict of truth and falsehood within it as the pledge of God's love, and to picture to itself faith, as a sort of passive quality which sits amid the ruins of human nature, and keeps up what may be called a silent protest, or indulges a pensive mediation over its misery. And, indeed, faith thus regarded cannot do more; for while it doesn't act to lead the soul to Christ, but to detain it from Him, how can the soul but remain a human prisoner, in that legal or natural state described by the Apostle Paul in Romans 7?

'True faith is what may be called colourless, like air or water; it's but the medium through which the soul sees Christ. There's a danger in Evangelical circles that people aim at experiences (as they are called) within them, rather than at Him Who is outside them.'

For some minutes now, I had had no wish to interrupt Newman. What he was saying fascinated me perhaps more than anything he had previously said. I think I now understood his view of justification (which of course he would claim was nothing new, or unique to him, but what the Catholic Church, at its best, had always taught). What he was saying shed light on all that he had previously said.

'Listen to what they say at "testimony meetings",' Newman suggested. 'Testimony givers are encouraged to enlarge upon the signs of conversion, the variations of their feelings, their aspirations and longings, and tell others how they feel, and hope, and sin, and rejoice, and renounce themselves, and rest in Christ only; how conscious they are that their best deeds are but "filthy rags" and all is of grace, till in fact they have little time left them to guard against what they are condemning and to exercise what they think they are so full of – faith. As true faith is so very different from self-contemplation it's no wonder that when the thought of self obscures the thought of God, prayer and praise languish; and the practice of simply contemplating our Maker, Redeemer, Sanctifier, and Judge is crowded out.

'To look at Christ is to be justified by faith; to think of being justified by faith is to look from Christ and fall from grace. He who worships Christ and works for Him is acting that doctrine which someone else just talks about; his worship and his works are acts of faith, and avail to his salvation because he does them as availing.

'The great moral of the history of Protestantism is this: Luther found in the Church great corruptions allowed by the highest authorities; he felt them; but instead of meeting them with divine weapons, he used one of his own. He adopted a doctrine original, specious, fascinating, persuasive, powerful against Rome, and wonderfully adapted as if prophetically to the genius of the times which were to follow.

'Luther found Christians in bondage to their works; he released them by his doctrine of faith; and he left them in bondage to their feelings. He weaned them from seeking assurance of salvation in standing ordinances, by teaching that a personal consciousness of it was promised to everyone who believed. For outward signs of grace he substituted inward; for reverence to the Church, contemplation of self. And thus, whereas he himself (unlike Zwingli) held the proper efficacy of the sacraments, he has led others to disbelieve it; whereas he preached against reliance on self, he introduced it in a more subtle shape; whereas he professed to make the written word all in all, he sacrificed it in its length and breadth to the doctrine he had wrested from a few texts.

'That's what comes of fighting God's battles in our own way, of extending truths beyond their measure, of anxiety after a teaching more compact, clear and spiritual than the Creed of the apostles.'

18   Enter the poet

There came a knock at the door and the Rev. Isaac Williams was announced. While Newman and he talked for a while in another room, Mozley briefed me on our visitor.

'Williams is a wonderful example of what the Oxford Movement can do. He came up from Harrow to Trinity College, a very finished Latin scholar and a first-rate cricketer, with no care for religion at all. Through winning the Latin Poem Prize he came to know Keble. That friendship changed his life. From then on, his faith meant everything to him. He became Fellow and Tutor of Trinity, and also for a while, Newman's curate at St Mary's.

'As a leading figure in the movement, he narrowly missed succeeding Keble as Professor of Poetry just a few weeks ago.

You'll find that he's everything that Ward isn't – quiet and shy, in fact he can never see a dozen people together without wanting to hide himself! But no one doubts his brilliance as a theologian and poet.

'In one of his poems, *The Baptistery*, Williams describes the relation between the actions of men in this life and the eternity which lies before them using the image of the cataract which freezes as it falls: some say that these lines are grander than the finest of Keble's, or even of Wordsworth's.

'Williams wrote three of the *Tracts for the Times* including two on what is known as "reserve in communicating Christian knowledge". As a firm believer in Newman's idea that faith is deepened and confirmed by moral growth, Williams argued in his tracts that the holiest mysteries of Christianity shouldn't be thrown into the market place of the profane, but should be communicated as men by moral development are able to receive them. But the title of these tracts was enough to spark off an almighty row: the very word "reserve" suggested keeping back part of the counsel of God. Enemies of the movement said it showed that the Oxford Movement loved secret and crooked ways and was Jesuitical in spirit. The Bishop of Gloucester roundly condemned the tracts without ever reading them.'

Newman and Williams joined us, closely followed by two Oriel servants who brought us lunch. In the presence of the author of the controversial tracts on reserve I decided not to miss an opportunity of asking a question which had troubled me since I had heard Newman preach.

'In your sermon yesterday,' I said, looking across the small table at Newman, 'you said that the doctrine of the atonement, though at the heart of religion, wasn't one to be talked of, but to be lived. You said that the doctrine shouldn't be used as a necessary instrument in the conversion of the ungodly, or to satisfy sceptics. Instead you said that it should be unfolded, if I remember your words correctly, to "the docile and obedient; to young children whom the world hasn't corrupted; to the sorrowful who need comfort;

107

to the sincere and earnest who need a rule for life; to the innocent who need a warning; and to the established, who have earned the knowledge of it". What did you mean when you said that?'

'Your memory is perfect,' said Newman with a smile. 'And how fortunate that dear Williams has joined us, for you may know that he contributed to our series of tracts on just this subject.'

Newman nodded at Williams.

'Well, the first thing I wanted to do in my tracts,' Williams began, 'was to show that in God's dealings with us, there is in fact a very remarkable holding back of sacred and important truths. It's as if the knowledge of them would hurt people unworthy of them. Having discussed this, I pointed out that some important practical reflections arise. I've no doubt that there is in fact a tendency on God's part to conceal and throw a veil over His truth, as if it would hurt us, unless we are in the right frame of mind to receive it.

'Of course the present mood in the world is against this principle of reserve. But if you study the whole religious system of the ancient Church and the works of the Fathers you'll find the principle is all-pervasive. However, in the present state of the world things are different: the art of printing brings home knowledge to all; the means which God formerly allowed to hide the knowledge of His truth are removed.

'Men of various creeds combine together in the circulation of the Scriptures. Add to this, we see preachers and teachers of various parties and from various motives, all busily engaged in imparting religious instruction.

'What are the general rules for the attainment of religious truth? With regard to preaching, George Herbert gives the following as qualifications for the preacher: "The character of his sermons is holiness; he is not witty, or learned, or eloquent, but holy . . . his library is 'a divine life'. Speech, therefore, with him is chiefly effective as the means by which the all prevailing force of example passes from one to another

. . . the only way to promote the good of others is to begin by self-discipline."'

19　True doctrine of the cross

'Now let's think,' said Williams, 'about the prevailing notion that it's necessary to bring forward the atonement *explicitly* and *prominently* on all occasions. It's evidently quite opposed to the teaching of Scripture, nor do we find any sanction for it in the gospels. If the epistles of Paul *appear* to be in favour of it, this is only at first sight. A key characteristic of Paul seems to have been a going out of himself to enter into the feelings and put himself in the circumstances of others.

'This accounts for the occasions on which Paul brings forward the doctrine of the atonement; as in the Epistles to the Romans and the Galatians. In both these cases, the prejudices which closed up the ears of his readers against the truth were opposed to the atonement. So much in the writings of Paul does the Holy Spirit adapt His teaching to the wants of each, as our Lord did in His incarnation.

'Also, Paul speaks of himself as at all times preaching "Christ crucified"; and Origen wrote that Christ crucified was the first doctrine taught, and that of our Lord's divinity the last which men knew. But this, in fact, so far from contradicting, strongly confirms my view; when Paul speaks in this way, it isn't the atonement and divinity of our Lord which he brings forward, although it's implied in his sayings. The whole of Paul's life and actions after his conversion, and the whole of his teaching, may be said to have been nothing other than a setting forth of Christ crucified, as the one great principle which absorbed all his heart, and motivated all his conduct. It's a great mistake to suppose that expressions like "Christ crucified" contain nothing more, or that, by preaching the atonement, we're preaching what Paul meant by Christ crucified.

'If you look carefully at the context in all the passages where these expressions occur, you'll see that Paul always intends the opposite meaning to the modern notion. It's the necessity of our being crucified to the world, it's our humiliation together with Him, mortification of the flesh, being made conformable to His sufferings and death. It was a doctrine which was "foolishness to the wise and an offence to the Jew" on account of the abasement of the natural man which it implies.

'On the other hand, the notion now prevailing is attractive to the world, in the naked way in which it's put forward, so as rather to diminish than to increase, a sense of responsibility and consequent humiliation.

'The doctrine of the atonement is conveyed in the expression Christ crucified, as used by Paul, but it's by teaching at the same time the necessity of our humiliation, which is repugnant to popular opinion today. It's expressing, in other words, our Saviour's declaration, "If anyone would come after me, he must deny himself and take up his cross daily and follow me" (Luke 9:23).

'And so both Paul and our Lord taught that we can't approach God without a sacrifice – a sacrifice on the part of human nature in union with that of our Saviour. The cross of Christ which Paul preached was that "through which the world has been crucified to me, and I to the world" (Gal. 6:14), "carrying around in our body the death of Jesus" (2 Cor. 4:10).

'And our Lord Jesus taught precisely the same truth. His own humiliation, and the necessity of our humiliation together with Him, was the doctrine signified by the cross which He put forward and presented to the people, in contrast to that of His own divinity, and our salvation through the same, which He rather kept secret.

'The doctrine of the atonement is secretly implied in the whole of Scripture. In the gospel it's in most of the precepts, in the blessings, in most of the parables, so much so that they would have no meaning without it as the foundation; for how

110

is the mourner to be comforted without it, or the poor in spirit to have the kingdom? How is the prodigal to be received with such a welcome, or what is the pearl of great price, and the hidden treasure?

'In the same way, it ought to pervade the teachings of the Church under the same spirit, as it does in its liturgies, especially the baptismal service. And as a fuller reception of this truth will accompany all growth in grace in a good man, proceeding from Christ crucified, to a broader, deeper, and higher sense of that atonement and our Lord's divinity, so will it pervade all His teaching under the same spirit.

'The apparent paradox which we witness of Christianity having become publicly acceptable to the world, contrary to our Lord's express declarations that it wouldn't be so acceptable, can only be accounted for by its having been put forward without its distinguishing characteristic, the humiliation of the natural man – the true doctrine of the cross having been hidden, or those truths connected with it which are most pleasing to men and women being brought forward alone.

'Every great doctrine of Scripture secretly pervades the whole of it under different forms, and in different degrees, and it's dangerous when we not only give an undue and exclusive prominence to any one truth, but bring forward that one singly and nakedly without all that which accompanies it in Scripture.'

'Doesn't the Christian idea of "revelation" contradict the idea of reserve?' I asked. 'Isn't the whole purpose of Scripture to communicate knowledge, not to conceal it? Surely the Bible reveals God's goodness to His creatures who are in darkness? Surely, whatever abstract principles you may hold, it's still our duty to preach the gospel of Christ crucified on every opportunity?'

'Doubtless we should,' Williams replied. 'A "dispensation is committed" to us to preach the gospel. In fact, though, the principle of reserve is in no way inconsistent with this duty – rather it's the more effective way of fulfilling it.

'Think of it this way. It's our duty to "let our light shine before men" (Matt. 5:16), to set a good example, that they "may see our good works"; but at the same time it's true that the great Christian rule of conduct, as the very foundation of all holiness, is that our religious actions should be in secret as far as possible. These two therefore are perfectly compatible. And unless we act on the principle of hiding our good works, our example will be quite useless.

'In the same way, our "preaching Christ crucified" will be without its proper effect, unless it's founded on this principle of natural modesty, which should always accompany the preaching of a good man.

"Why should all the truths of religion be taught at once? In all other areas there is a gradual instruction: something must be withheld, something taught first; and isn't the knowledge of religion as much a matter of degree as any human science? I don't lower the doctrine of the atonement, but heighten and exalt it – all I say is that it should be looked upon and spoken of with reverential holiness.'

20 Why people reject reserve

'Let's think,' said Williams, 'about that popular system of religion which turns people against the doctrine of reserve. It's a system which is characterised by these features: the notion that it's necessary to bring forward prominently and explicitly on all occasions the doctrine of the atonement: this one thing it puts in the place of all the principles held by the Church Catholic, getting things out of balance.

'Popular religion disparages, in some cases has even blasphemed, the sacraments. It's afraid of Church authority, of fasting and mortification, of works of holiness being insisted on, of the doctrine of the universal judgment. It's marked by an unreserved discourse on the holiest subjects.

'Now this system differs fundamentally from what is

Catholic: by the term Catholic I mean a combination of what both the universal Church and the Bible teaches, the former as interpreting the latter. I do believe that popular, so-called Evangelical religion is unscriptural, un-Catholic, unreal. I've no doubt that this maxim of reserve is directly opposed to it throughout.

'I believe that advocates of the Evangelical system set aside much of the Bible, including the gospels themselves. They quote only some parts of Scripture for their purposes. Their views are not according to the general tenor or the analogy of Scripture, nor are they founded or based on Scripture as their origin.

'They think there's something particularly life-giving and heart-searching in this style of preaching which thrusts forth exclusively and indiscriminately the doctrine of the atonement, and proclaims loudly the necessity of our dependence on the Holy Spirit. These doctrines are considered in distinction from those doctrines which also recommend practical duties, and various forms of public and private religious worship.

'It's certainly true that a more adequate sense of the atonement – broader, higher, and deeper views of the mystery which is "hid in Christ" – is indeed the perfection of the Christian character. Advancement in holiness is a continual progress in self-abasement and self-renunciation towards that repose which is in God "manifested in Jesus Christ".

'And the same is true with respect to the idea that it's necessary to name always the ever-blessed Spirit of God; certainly the same gradual perfection of a Christian will consist in a deeper and continually increasing sense of his utter inability to support himself in spiritual life, and a confidence that he can do all things through Christ strengthening him; a feeling of thorough dependence on God every moment of his existence, not only in sustaining his natural, but much more the new and regenerate life.

'But how is this state to be obtained? These peculiar opinions are formed on the assumption that it's by declaring these truths aloud to all we meet. This is the point on which we differ. For this there's no sanction in all the laws of our moral nature and religious philosophy; there's none for it in the Catholic Church, none in the Bible.

'If we are to look out for some practical guide to know in what way we are to hold and declare scriptural doctrine, surely it's our duty to bring forward "the faith once for all delivered unto the saints" in the fullness of that Creed into which we were baptised. Isn't this the divinely appointed guardian by which we may keep what is contained in Scripture in its right balance, which has been given us as a key to the right understanding of Scripture, and also an authoritative statement of what in doctrine we are to hold and teach? For of course if we put forward one truth to the exclusion of others, the effect of our teaching may be equivalent to falsehood, and not truth.

'I'm sure that the preparations of the heart which can alone receive the faith in its fullness are by other means than those which this system supposes; Scripture and reason both would imply that it's by insisting first of all on natural piety, on the necessity of common honesty, on repentance, on judgment to come, and without any way of speaking that excepts ourselves from that judgment – by urging those helps to poverty of spirit, which Scripture recommends and the Church prescribes, such as fasting and alms, and the necessity of reverent and habitual prayer.

'These are the means of bringing people to the truth as it is in Jesus Christ, with that awe and fear, which our Lord's own teaching and that of His apostles would inspire. Surely we should be careful not to be deceiving ourselves and others by an irreverent handling of God's most sacred consolations.

'People say that we should bring forward the doctrine of the atonement on all occasions, prominently and exclusively. But I'm quite at a loss to know on what grounds they think this. Is it from its supposed effects? Pious frauds might be supported on the same principle: but consider these effects. The fruits of the system have shown themselves in the disobedience of ministers to their ecclesiastical superiors, of individuals to their appointed ministers, of whole bodies of Christians to the Church. Is it the popularity of the opinion? This isn't a test of truth, but an argument to the contrary; Christian truth is in itself essentially unpopular; and even were it otherwise, what is popularity when it's opposed to Catholic antiquity? Is it from Scripture? The tone and spirit of the Bible is quite opposed to it.'

'So, are you saying,' I asked, 'that we should never mention the atonement in public?'

'I've never suggested anything of the sort,' Williams replied, still looking at me, and occasionally at Newman and Mozley, with his endearingly shy and modest smile. 'That would of course be as unnatural as the other approach. Why shouldn't we be content to act naturally, with the Church and Scripture as our guides? Or, if we may reverently use such words, why shouldn't we act as the Holy Spirit, ever enlightening the path of obedience, dictates to us?

'Some say: aren't we saved by faith in Christ alone, and if so, what else have we to preach? I answer by another question: wasn't it the very work of John the Baptist to be the herald of Christ, and yet, so little did he publicly make a practice of declaring this that there was a doubt whether he was not himself the Christ: but instead of proclaiming Him aloud, he taught repentance, and to each individual amendment of life. The Baptist declared, "I came that He might be manifested," but how was He to be made known, except, as our Lord said, that He would make Himself known to him that kept His commandments. Therefore the forerunner preached repentance.

'When John the Baptist did allude to the atonement, in the expression "the Lamb of God Who takes away the sin of the world" it was secretly and obscurely, and probably only to a few chosen and favoured disciples, who themselves couldn't have understood the clear meaning of the allusion, to whom it must have been a dark saying.

'Doubtless we are saved by faith in Christ alone; but to

115

come to know this in all its power, is the very perfection of the Christian; not to be instilled or obtained by lifting up the voice in the street, but by obedience and penitence, so that, as each man advances in holiness of life, and comes more and more to know what God is, the more does he feel himself, with the saints of all ages, to be the chief of sinners.

'But as for that assurance and confidence with which it is thought necessary the doctrine should be preached and received, surely all those who are recorded in Scripture as being most approved, were remarkable for the absence of this confidence; as in the case of the Centurion, the Canaanite woman, and others. Remember those who at the last day will be surprised with the welcome news that they are accepted, while those who are rejected will come with the plea of confidence, because they've prophesied in Christ's name, and He has taught in their street: they'll be condemned with emphatic words, as they that work iniquity.

'The whole stress is so often thrown on that single point, which those who hold these opinions are careful to make of secondary importance, the necessity of working righteousness (for example, Matt. 7:21–3; 25:31–46).

'Surely the doctrine of the atonement may be taught in all its fullness, on all occasions, and all seasons, more effectively, more really, and truly, according to the proportion of the faith, or the need of circumstances, without being brought out from the context of Holy Scripture into prominent and explicit mention. Didn't James preach the gospel most effectively under the guidance of the Holy Spirit? Didn't Paul preach the gospel to the Thessalonians when he spoke of the day of judgment, as well as to the Galatians when, in answer to certain Jewish prejudices, he said that the only remission of sins was to be found in the cross of Christ?

'May we not regulate our teachings according to the condition of the person we address, as they did? But above all, didn't our Lord preach the gospel? Didn't He say to the two disciples who came from John the Baptist, "To the poor the gospel is preached" (Matt. 11:5)? But how was it preached?

'We know what the preaching of Jesus was: He taught the atonement always, but never openly. He taught it in the beatitudes, in the parables, in His miracles, in His commands, in His warnings, in His promises; He taught it always, but always covertly, never at all in the manner now practised, but quite the opposite.

'And as it pervaded all our Lord's teaching, and ought to do the teaching of every Christian, so surely it may do so in a way to be more effectively impressed on others, and to indicate its thorough reception into the character of the speaker, by one who might have even never prominently and explicitly declared it, any more than our Lord does in His own teaching. It may be impressed on others by the tone of a person's whole thoughts, by the silent instruction of his penitent and merciful manner, by immediate inference and implication from his sayings, by the only interpretation which his words will bear; but above all things, by the doctrine of the sacraments always influencing his life. In this way the preacher may always bear about in his body the marks of the Lord Jesus, and preach Christ crucified.

'The important thing needed are those preparations of the heart which may lead men to humiliation and contrition; when this is done, He who "dwells with the humble and the contrite" will never fail to lead them to all the consolation of religion.

'Imagine that a friend consults us about something that troubles his conscience: how tender and careful should we be in such a case for fear of administering comfort too speedily, lest by so doing we check the workings of God's Holy Spirit, and heal too slightly His wounds to our friend's great detriment?

'But besides this, the awful name of the blessed Spirit, without whom we can neither think nor do anything that is right, is, it is now thought, to be proclaimed as it were in the market-place, and those who don't do so are supposed to deny His power, the power of the ever-blessed Spirit of God, in Whose name we were baptised, Whom in the doxology we

117

confess daily, in Whom we live and move. Let these sacred words be introduced in our teaching, as they are in Scripture. But we must be careful that they aren't used in an unreal manner, and "taken in vain". For these holiest of words may be constantly used by us, when we aren't at all affected and influenced by so concerning a doctrine, which may be seen by the whole of our character in daily life, and tone of our teaching; by self-confidence, and an absence of that fear and trembling which always follows the consciousness that it's God that works in us both to will and to do.

'There's great danger in forming a plan of our own, different from that of Scripture. Surely we don't know what we do when we venture to make a scheme and system of our own respecting the revelations of God. His ways are so vast and mysterious, that there may be some great presumption in our taking one truth and forming around it a scheme from notions of our own.

'We sometimes hear sermons which are throughout plausible, which seem at first sight scriptural, and are received as such without hesitation, and yet, on a little consideration, we see that they're partial views of the truth, that they are quite inconsistent with the much forgotten doctrine of a future judgment.

'The Evangelical scheme puts knowledge first, and obedience afterwards: let this doctrine, they say, be received, and good works will necessarily follow. Scripture throughout adopts the opposite approach. The language it adopts, and the plan it pursues, is on the principle that "the law was our schoolmaster to bring us unto Christ" (Gal. 3:24 AV) that "if any man will do his will, he shall know of the doctrine" (John 7:17 AV); whereas this teaching is "receive only this doctrine, and you will do the will".

'The kind of secondary way in which the need for obedience is put in the Evangelical system is the very opposite of scriptural teaching. Scripture always introduces the warning clause, "if you keep the commandments"; they, on the contrary, say "if you don't think of them too much".'

I understood what Williams was saying on this point. Because Evangelicals make much of the grace of God which saves us they tend to put God's grace and human effort in opposition to one another. So 'keeping the commandments' and 'law' are associated with the old covenant, and 'freedom' is associated with the new; thus people are given the impression that they shouldn't think too much about the commandments. But this muddled thinking is by no means universal among Evangelicals: I recalled recently attending a service at Oxford's stronghold of Evangelicalism, St Aldate's church, where the sermon was one of a series on the ten commandments.

'Isn't there,' Williams asked, 'an extraordinary confusion and perplexity raised which has the effect of entangling men's minds with words and phrases? Christian repentance is sometimes spoken of as something not only separate from, but opposed to Christ. The effect of Christian good works is treated as having a tendency to puff up with pride and selfishness: works of humility and charity, exercised in secret, purely with the desire of pleasing God, for of course these are the only sort of works which could be insisted on (though of course what they mean must be bad works, those of hypocrisy).

'Or again, they say that religious services weaken our dependence on the Holy Spirit; or, in other words, that frequent and constant prayers to God for His assistance, diminish our reliance on God. They say that the deep and awful sense of judgment to come detracts from Christ's atonement, as if the most earnest consideration of the former didn't most impress the unspeakable worth of the latter. Or again, that to insist on the value of the sacraments is to detract from Christ; for when it is considered that there is no value whatever supposed in those sacraments, except from Christ's presence in them, and His atoning blood communicated through them, this is precisely the same as if a similar charge were brought against attaching too high a value to the Scriptures; for it might be said we put the Scriptures in place of Christ.'

119

21   Good works and the atonement

'To answer those who oppose the idea of reserve,' Williams
said, 'we must refer to plain first axioms in morals. Religious
doctrines and articles of faith can only be received in a certain
state of heart; this state of heart can only be formed by a
repetition of certain actions.

'According to Aristotle, the perception of any moral truth
depends on the life which a person leads. He says that it
depends on our intellect itself, as in pure science; but that the
understanding must have combined with it a certain desire,
love, or motive; but this desire or motive depends on the
mode of life and is given by it. Aristotle also says that that
which is truly good doesn't appear except to him who leads a
good life; and at another time that a man must be brought up
well to understand morals; and that vice destroys the faculty
of discerning truth. So on this view, if any article of the Creed
is less received than another, it's owing to some peculiarity
in the life and conduct either of an individual or an age that
rejects it.

'Therefore only a certain course of action can dispose us
to receive certain doctrines; and these doctrines are preached
in vain, unless these actions are at the same time practised
and insisted on as essential. For instance, charitable works
alone will make a man charitable, and the more anyone does
charitable works, the more charitable will he become; that's
to say, the more he'll love his neighbour and love God; for
a charitable work is a work that proceeds from charity or the
love of God, and which can only be done in the power of the
Holy Spirit; and the more he does these works therefore the
more he'll love his neighbour and love God; and he who
doesn't (in heart and intention at least) perform these works
won't be a charitable man, that is, won't love God or his
neighbour.

'He therefore will most of all love God and love Christ
who does these works most; and he will bring men to Christ,

who most effectively, with God's blessing, induces them to do these works in the way that God has required them to be done.

'Or again, only he will be humble in heart who does humble actions; and no action is (morally speaking) a humble action except one which proceeds from the spirit of humility; and he who does humble actions most will be most humble; and he who is most humble will be most emptied of self-righteousness, and therefore will most value the cross of Christ, being least of all conscious of his own good deeds; and the more he does these works, the more will the Holy Spirit dwell with him, according to the promises of Scripture, and the more fully will he come to the knowledge of that mystery which is hid in Christ.

'So that teacher who will most induce men to good works, will most of all bring men to Christ, though he doesn't speak fully and loudly of His ever blessed atonement.

'Or again, good works consist especially in prayers. He who prays most seeks most of all for an assistance out of and beyond himself, and therefore relies least of all on himself and most of all on God. And the more he does this, the more he relies upon God's Holy Spirit, for which he asks. Therefore he who, by preaching the judgment to come, or by recommending alms and fasting, or by impressing men with a sense of the shortness of life and the value of eternity, will lead men most to pray, will do most towards leading them to lean on God's Holy Spirit, although he may not repeat in express words the necessity of aid from that Spirit without Whom men can't please God.

'To say therefore that such works, which alone are good works, tend to foster pride, and are seeking for expiations beyond the one great atonement, conveys a most dangerous fallacy; when the works which are intended must be bad works, those of ostentation, of hypocrisy, or superstition, and the like, which, of course, the more often they are repeated, the more do they make men ostentatious, hypocritical, or superstitious; and so take them from the cross of Christ. They are sins against which we cannot warn men too much; sins repeatedly condemned by Christ, Who never condemns or disparages good works, but always insists upon them most earnestly. Let hypocrisy in all its shapes be condemned as Scripture condemns, and we shall fully understand such teaching.

'We can say the same about the love of praise; or about purity of heart: for a man of impure heart may be very affected by the touching and vital doctrines of the gospel and yet he can't receive them rightly; for the pure in heart alone can see God; and therefore can alone see, so as rightly to understand, those doctrines in which God is made known. That minister, therefore, who, by preaching the terrors of the judgment day, or by any other scriptural means, induces men to repent of these crimes, will necessarily open their eyes, their ears, their heart, to receive the high saving principles of the gospel; though he speaks not explicitly of them any more than the Baptist did, or our Lord, or His apostles.

'So it's absurd, even on the plain grounds of moral principles, to speak of the teaching of repentance being opposed to the preaching of Christ. So often, the Bible connects our own cross with the cross of Christ; for Jesus said, "anyone who does not take his cross and follow me is not worthy of me" (Matt. 10:38).

'Now there can be no repentance, and no progress in religious duties, without self-denial. These duties therefore are a bearing of our own cross, which will alone bring us to a right sense of the cross of Christ, not disparaging it; it's only showing the mode by which alone we may be brought to know its inestimable value.

'He who most of all practises these duties will be most of all brought to value the cross of Christ; and he who is brought to embrace that doctrine with most affection, will speak of it with most reserve; he cannot speak of it as these people do.'

I noticed Mozley fidgeting and looking increasingly irritable. Newman sat listening impassively. I wondered how

122

well the Oxford Movement's teaching on reserve had been received.

'Good works,' Isaac Williams continued, 'are nothing other than the exercise of a good principle; they will make a good man (as far as, humanly speaking, a man can be called good), and those aren't good works which won't make a man good; and he isn't a good man who doesn't love God with all his heart, and depend on the aid of the Holy Spirit, and trust in Christ.

'Therefore he who most of all encourages men to practise good works, under the awful sense of their condition as baptised Christians, brings them most of all to the cross of Christ; and he who, by his teaching, leads men to think that such works are of minor importance, and speaks slightingly of them, that is works of charity, of humiliation, and prayer, teaches men false and dangerous doctrine. Their teaching flatters human indolence, but opposes Scripture, opposes the Church, and opposes the first principles of our moral nature.

'That's why our Lord said, "Anyone who breaks one of the least of these commandments and teaches others to do the same will be called least in the kingdom of heaven" (Matt. 5:19); in other words, he who treats slightingly these good works, shall obtain the least of all the blessings of Christ's spiritual kingdom at present, the gracious gifts which are in the atonement of Christ, and by consequence be the lowest in His kingdom hereafter.

'By using high words of doctrine, without the teaching of these commands, we lead men to trust a vain shadow, instead of the rock of their salvation.

'Doing the works or not is that which makes the difference between the house built on the sand, and that which is founded on a rock, though outwardly they appear the same; as our Lord has warned, he who "hears these words of mine and puts them into practice is like a wise man who built his house on the rock" (Matt. 7:24); and "everyone who hears these words of mine and does not put them into

123

practice is like a foolish man who built his house on the sand" (Matt. 7:26).

'And what is the rock on which the wise man builds, but Christ? His very works are built on this rock, otherwise they aren't good works. It isn't as if Christ was the end only (as they who would disparage baptism would imply); not as if the atonement were a thing to be arrived at last; but Christ is the way also, the beginning and the end, the author and the finisher, the alpha and omega.

'It's only through the blood of Christ that we're able to think or do what is good. It's through His blood alone that our deeds are accepted. It's not simply that by bearing our cross we are brought to Him; but we are in Him, and He in us; our cross is His cross, and His cross is our cross. When we humble ourselves, we share in the virtue which issues from His humiliation: it's He that is drawing us nearer to Himself.

'When we pray it's not our prayer, but His Holy Spirit within us that leads us to Him. When we do works of charity, it's to Him in His brethren: it's His compassionate heart longing in us towards them: it's the virtue of His ineffable charity through us, His members again flowing out to all mankind. To discourage such works by any misstatements, by half admonitions and half encouragements, is to keep men from Him.

'It's true that in the gospels the consolations of Christ may be more imparted to people who were designated "sinners"; that "the tax collectors and the prostitutes are entering the kingdom of God ahead of you" (Matt. 21:31): but why? Not because they were worse, but because they were far better than the hypocritical Pharisees.

'The whole harmony of scriptural teaching is opposed to the present system, or what is sometimes designated the gospel scheme; the scriptural system, in contrast to the modern system, is one of reserve. We have shown, from obvious moral inference, that to correct the heart and practice is the only way to arrive at those riches which are hid in Christ.

124

'Surely a little reflection will show how thoroughly the Bible supports this opinion. Think of the way in which the commandments are spoken of, and that not merely in the New Testament, but in the Old also.

'Could words be applied to the commandments such as we find throughout the Psalms, for instance, unless they had some mysterious connection with the cross of Christ? How else could God's commands be "sweeter than honey, than honey from the comb" (Ps. 19:10)? How else could they be "more precious than thousands of pieces of silver and gold" (Ps. 119:72)? How else could they be "wonderful" (Ps. 119:129) and "preserving" (Ps. 119:25), "giving light to the eyes" (Ps. 19:8) and "for ever right" (Ps. 119:144)?

'If we consider the expressions by which the gospel privileges are spoken of in Scripture, we shall find that they are all connected with certain dispositions and graces, and confined to them. Those dispositions and graces can alone be attained by a certain mode of life and course of action. And Scripture teaches these actions by bringing before us every example, and precept, and doctrine, that may be calculated to affect us with the terrors of God's judgments, or the hopes of His mercy.

'Who does Scripture say are blessed? You might think from the modern system that the expression was "Blessed are all those of you who hear the gospel", and that this gospel is confined to a full declaration of the doctrine of the atonement; but that isn't how the Bible speaks. Jesus certainly said to some, "blessed are your eyes because they see, and your ears because they hear" (Matt. 13:16) – but then this wasn't said to all the people to whom our Lord had been preaching, but to the disciples "privately" as distinct from those who had heard our Lord teaching, but who, as He said, had no "eyes to see, nor ears to hear". In His more public teaching, His blessing was entirely confined and limited to certain attitudes of heart which are recorded in the Sermon on the Mount.

'To suppose therefore that a doctrine so unspeakable and mysterious as the atonement is to be held out to the impenitent sinner, to be embraced in some way to move the affections, is quite unlike our Lord's conduct.

'If we take the mere general outline and first view of the gospel narrative, it's so like all God's revelations of Himself to the world, and the history of what the Church was to be. "The desired of all nations" (Hag. 2:7) had come, "the messenger of the covenant, whom you desire" (Mal. 3:1); but He was to be "like a refiner's fire" (Mal. 3:2).

'We hardly know what we speak of when we speak of the atonement: it's a vast sea which no man can fathom. Who can think of it worthily? Who can comprehend the sacraments in which it's hidden? Surely men don't know what they do when they define and systematise the ways of God in man's redemption, under expressions such as imputed righteousness, justification and sanctification. These words stand in their minds for some exceeding shallow poor human ideas for which they vehemently contend, as for the whole of religion. This is in fact to explain the inexpressible, to measure the infinite, to enter into the secret counsels of God. Actually we know nothing whatever except this: that a childlike obedience which accepts the commands of Scripture will be brought to the full knowledge of God.

'Doubtless we may suppose that our Lord went about in the fullness of the power of the atonement (if we may so speak) out of that vast sea of mercy, dispensing to men as they were able to receive it. What were the bodily cures that He wrought, connected as they were with the forgiveness of sins; and what the various blessings that He pronounced? Those gifts were distributed according as the dispositions of men made them capable of receiving them. To one it was the kingdom of heaven, to another it was consolation, to another it was righteousness, to another it was mercy, to another it was the power of God.

'In this way the unspeakable power of the atonement was in the beatitudes distributed according to each man's obedience. Not as gifts falling from heaven in the cup of each; but in every case as a pearl of great price, as hidden treasure.

126

To another it is spoken of as "refreshment", to another as "rest for the soul", to another as being to Jesus Christ as "brother and sister and mother", to another that God the Father and Jesus Christ would "make our home with him" (John 14:23). But observe on each of these occasions how perfectly mysterious and secret the gift is; how closely limited and restricted to certain attitudes of heart; how on every occasion the conditions are put first, the attitude required, or the keeping of the commandments, and the gifts following: in short, these promises and privileges vouchsafed to the Christian are distributed in a manner much like the miracles, which were apparently dispensed by an invariable law according to the faith of each. And both of them on a principle quite opposed to these modern opinions, which speak of "the display of God's mercy in the atonement".

'On all occasions, the very opposite conduct is pursued to that of the human system. The Lord of heaven and earth, in the full power of His divinity and atoning mercy, but ever as it were hiding Himself, as a poor man going about with a few fishermen, calling everyone that came to Him to privation and hardship, putting these as it were always first, and keeping back the blessing; checking men and setting aside their wish to follow Him when they expected anything but hardship; as when to one man He said, "Foxes have holes and birds of the air have nests, but the Son of Man has nowhere to lay his head" (Luke 9:58); or demanding an instant surrender without delay, as of him to whom He said, "Let the dead bury their own dead, but you go and proclaim the kingdom of God" (Luke 9:60).

'And notice the rich man on whom Jesus looked and "loved him" (Mark 10:21) and who seemed not to understand the true nature of the gospel; how differently did our Lord treat him to the way these modern religionists would require us to act, when He called on him to practise the most self-denying duties and the exercise of charity.

'And notice how all these gifts in which the kingdom of heaven consists are attached to these conditions, and inseparable from them: so that to have the appropriate attitude, or to fulfil the commands required, is in that degree to partake of the spiritual blessings; and not to fulfil them is to miss out on those gifts. We are commanded to learn of Christ to be "gentle and humble in heart" and we will find rest for our souls (Matt. 11:29): so far as we become gentle and humble in heart we shall find rest to our souls; and this rest is not given to any except so far as they are so.

'Christ says that if we keep His commandments He will come and make His home with us, and so far as we keep the commandments, we shall certainly have Christ living with us; and so far as He lives with us, we shall of course be partakers of all the privileges of the gospel as a necessary and infallible consequence (John 14:21–3).

'The same argument may be applied to every blessing in the gospels: for instance, the poor in spirit does naturally and of necessity come to the enjoyment of the Christian inheritance; whatever teaching therefore disengages men from the love of wealth will bring them so far into their Christian inheritance; every act which produces this spirit, leads men one step into the possession of this their Christian birthright.

'You see how fully the scriptural statements confirm everything I've said about actions and habits; that actions alone can produce the right attitude of heart, and attitudes alone can receive doctrines. Or to put it another way, all knowledge of saving doctrine is revealed from above to those who will do God's will. For every act of obedience is rewarded by God with additional light, and the fullness of this light, illuminating the path of obedience, is the knowledge of God. So that in whatever way we consider it, there's no scriptural sanction for the necessity of our always thrusting forward the doctrine of the atonement without reserve.'

22 Obtaining eternal life

'You can see the same harmony of Scripture,' Williams said, 'in the variety of ways in which the Bible refers to the one thing that's needed in order to obtain eternal life. In one place it says, "Believe in the Lord Jesus, and you will be saved" (Acts 16:31). Whereas in another place our Lord says "If you want to enter life, obey the commandments" (Matt. 19:17). So that these two requirements will necessarily imply each other, and somehow to keep the commandments will lead us to Christ, and will be believing in Him.

'But the commandments contain the love of God and the love of our neighbour; and to know this principle, the spiritual interpretations of the commandments, our Lord told the lawyer, was to be "not far from the kingdom of God" (Mark 12:34). And this was the test which our Lord put to the rich young man whom He loved, telling him to give to the poor and follow Him. These two points, therefore, in this case, would indicate whether he had kept the commandments or understood the spirit of them.

'In the same way, Paul tells us that faith will profit us nothing, and works will profit us nothing, without love, which alone avails (1 Cor. 13). On the other hand John tells us that to know God is eternal life; and therefore faith, and obedience, and love and knowledge must in some sense be one and the same, or necessarily imply each other. For if we keep the commandments we shall enter into life; and so also if we believe in Christ, or know Christ, it's eternal life. And yet no one of these is without the other.

'If therefore God's promises are so diverse, may not our teaching reflect this variety of God's Word, without our being bound to use a human system? And why may not those who teach love and obedience lead men to the truth?

'Surely it's sufficient to say that we are following the method of Scripture: nor can anything else be truly said to reflect the richness of God's Word. This surely is the way to "proclaim to you the whole will of God" (Acts 20:26).

'It's he who humbles himself most, and obeys most dutifully, who attains most of all to a right and saving sense of the atonement of Christ. And thus we come again to the same point with regard to our teaching – that he who most of all impresses himself and others with a sense of the day of judgment, will most of all lead himself and others to keep the commandments; and he who does this will be the most humble, and will most of all embrace the doctrine of the atonement; whereas he who puts forward this doctrine most prominently, in a different way than the general teaching of God's Word, may be taking people furthest from it.

'Again, we have said the necessary effect of keeping the commandments is to empty a man of self-righteousness, and therefore to bring him to Christ crucified. Now this might be shown in all the examples of holy men of Scripture; for whatever other graces they might have, they are marked with humility. Thus the Apostle Paul, because he had always laboured to have a "conscience clear before God and man" (Acts 24:16) and in the gospel had "worked harder" than all the apostles (1 Cor. 15:10), therefore felt himself the chief of sinners.

'Holy men have always loved much because they felt they had much forgiven; and they felt they had much forgiven because they loved much. So far therefore as we keep the commandments we shall embrace the atonement, and so far only, whether we speak of it or not.

'But how very inconsistent with this is the attitude which this system has introduced, of judging of the saints of God according to how far and how much they speak of the atonement! Think what great injury is done to a generation who are taught to disparage the saints of the primitive church who spent their days and nights in frequent prayers, in fastings, and mortification, and retirement from the world. Men have been induced to believe that this was not merely a circuitous and difficult way to obtain the favour of God, but that these saints of God have failed to find the right and saving way altogether!'

23   Promoting Christianity

'So,' I asked Williams, 'how important is preaching in the life of the Church?'

'Well,' he replied, 'I think Evangelicals generally break the spirit of reserve by attaching so great a value to preaching as to disparage the Prayer Book and sacraments in comparison. According to them, the Church of God would be the House of Preaching whereas Scripture calls it the House of Prayer.

'In the present day it's taken for granted that eloquence in speech is the most powerful means of promoting religion in the world. But if this is the case, it's remarkable that there's no hint of this in Scripture; perhaps no single expression can be found in any part of it that implies it: there's no recommendation of rhetoric in precept, or example, or prophecy. There's no instance of it; no part of Scripture itself looks as if it's the remains of what was delivered with powerful eloquence.

'If people in general were asked what was the most powerful means of advancing the cause of religion in the world, we should be told that it was eloquence of speech or preaching: and the excellence of speech we know consists in delivery. Whereas, if we read the Bible to discover the best means of promoting Christianity in the world, we find that it's obedience; and if we were to be asked the second, we should say obedience; and if we were asked the third we should say obedience. If the spirit of obedience exists, simple and calm statement of truth will go far.

'Not that I'm entirely belittling preaching as a mode of doing good; but it's a characteristic of the Evangelical system as opposed to that of the Church that it gives preaching more emphasis than I believe it is given in Scripture.'

I thought about the prominent position given to wide, raised platforms placed centrally at the front of nonconformist chapels compared with the much smaller pulpits located less conspicuously at one side in Anglican churches.

'What's the effect of preaching?' Williams asked, warming to his theme. 'It brings people together in crowds and creates strong religious impressions: so far this may be good. But does preaching make men more keen to learn, and more exacting in adhering to truth? Does it make men more humble and obedient to their appointed ministers, more frequent in attending the daily prayers, more honest and just in their dealings with those around them? Does preaching lead men to think more of God and His demands on us and less of men and their gifts? Does it produce a healthy reverence for the sacraments? Are people who have been used to popular preaching more submissive to God's laws, and more easily moved to the self-denying duties of repentance and prayer? Certainly the silence of Scripture should make us cautious about the importance we attach to preaching.

'The great emphasis placed on these means is sufficient to show the tendency of the system; I'm afraid it's one of expediency, it looks to man: that of the Church is one of faith, and looks to God. Their principle is to speak much and loud, because it is to man; that of the Church is founded on this, that "God is in heaven and you are on earth", therefore "Guard your steps when you go to the house of God" and "let your words be few" (Ecc. 5:1,2).

'Those who profess principles holier, or wiser, or purer than those of Holy Scripture, do ultimately tend to the virtual denial of those very truths which they profess most strictly to uphold. Those who maintain that the Church doesn't sufficiently preach the dependence of man upon God, and trust in the atonement, do practically in their whole system tend to detract from those truths themselves, while the Church continues to hold them.'

This seemed an excessively harsh judgment on Evangelicalism, at least as far as the twentieth century was concerned, and perhaps, judging from Mozley's still irritated expression, as regards the nineteenth century too.

'They consider, for instance,' Williams added, 'that the efficacy of a preacher consists in human eloquence and activity, and not in the power of his divine commission. By disparaging the efficacy of the sacraments, they have come to substitute for them something like a meritorious act, or opinion, on the part of an individual. Professing to be guided exclusively by the written word, they have established a method so opposed to it, as to render the greater part of it superfluous. Requiring us to speak loudly of spiritual assistance, they have set at nought all those practices, whose sole end and object was to live in that invisible world, and to partake of its gifts.

'For men have been led to censure and even ridicule not the superstitious and wrong observances of sacramental ordinances, creeds, and prayers, but the punctual observance of them at all; and they say things which would brand with superstition the devout Daniel for his unbending adherence to times and circumstances of devotion; and the widow Anna, who departed not from the temple, with formalism. And all this arises from the fact that these opinions aren't thoroughly and unreservedly based on the Bible, and therefore look too much to external support.

'The very principle of sound religion is that the world "does not know us as it did not know him" (1 John 3:1): its rules of action are so essentially opposed that the world and sound religion cannot understand each other. The system of which we speak always has the indirect object of making a league with the world (though it would deny this and its followers may speak against worldliness); and it has substituted for the Church system a great unreal system, nominal, superficial, formal – though they claim it's spiritual.

'Where God is, there must be the fear of Him. For this reason it has come about that names of the most awful and holy importance have been so used habitually, that they don't carry with them their own high and awful meaning, even the names of the ever-blessed Trinity. Not only have they become used without reverence, and very much as the distinctive signs of a party – but the very use of them tends to keep up this feeling of unreality, and without bearing on the heart and conduct. Whereas homely natural expressions in which anyone who is in earnest is apt to clothe his sentiments, and which touch the heart and conscience of another, as they come from his own, are disliked; because they break this unreal web, and bear more on the daily life and conscience.

'All this is substituting a system of man's own creation for that which God has given. Instead of the sacraments and external ordinances, it has put forward prominently a supposed sense of the atonement, as the badge of profession. That which is most thoroughly internal, most thoroughly spiritual, secret, and holy, it has made the external symbol of agreement; and therefore has completely (so to speak) turned people inside out, wherever it is received: and so it has lost the essential peculiarity of Christianity, that purity of heart which is directed to the Father "who sees what is done in secret" (Matt. 6:4).

'For a time the earnestness of mind of this new system carried with it incidentally much good, and led men to embrace other great truths of Christianity, and perhaps that of Christ crucified, in reality as well as in name. Being far better themselves than their system, and better in practice than in their opinions, which they held rather speculatively and controversially; but now we often see the legitimate fruits of the system. The evils it has led to in various forms of dissent are too evident wherever we turn our eyes, leading men to the neglect of honesty and plain dealing, and at length to indifference, unsettledness and infidelity.

'The Evangelical system tends to exclude everything that may alarm the conscience of those who heartily adopt it, obedience to Church authority, practices of mortification, the fear of God, and the doctrine of judgment to

134

come. It sets forth religion in colours attractive to the world, by stimulating the affections, and by stifling the conscience, rather than by purifying and humbling the heart. Hence its great popularity in fashionable places. Instead of the process of painful self-discipline and gradual restoration, or the open and salutary penance of the ancient Church, this new system affords an instant route to arriving at the privileges and authority of advanced piety. And the consequence is that real humility of heart, and a quiet walking in the ordinances of God, finds not only the world in array against it, but that which considers itself as Christianity also.

'The system is marked by a lack of reverence; and therefore it can use worldly instruments and worldly organs. It may serve as a ready cloak to cover an unsubdued temper and a worldly spirit, concealing them as much from the individual himself as from others. One or two truths are put forward exclusively as the whole of religion. The present age likes to take all that is agreeable and beautiful and benevolent in Christianity, and reject what is stern and self-denying and awful.

'Now we have the truth of Christianity in its proper balance in the Creed, which God has given us as a key to Scripture, a guide and safeguard to each individual. But if we take one point only in religion, instead of the whole breadth of the faith, we produce a religion which may please ourselves and others, and yet may be very far from the truth as it is in the Bible, and from the principles of that new world where righteousness lives.'

24   The remedy of reserve

'Now against all this worldly system,' Williams said, 'the reserve that I and others advocate seems the remedy. It strips off all those external indications of a religion which doesn't exist in the heart; these external things hinder rather than promote true piety. We have nothing to show to ourselves or others to encourage the notion that we are better than they; reserve induces us to cultivate a sincere desire to be approved in the eyes of our Father "who sees in secret".

'A lack of reserve, an artificial religious tone in conversation or prayer, is a proof that the person is wishing to persuade himself that he is religious, rather than that he really is religious. As far as anyone is in earnest, he will act naturally with this sacred modesty, seeking to know God and do His will. This unaffected reserve will be a great protection to him in keeping the spirit of piety fresh and true, and when he loses it, he will lose half his strength.

'This secret devotion will doubtless lower him in his own eyes, and in the eyes of the world, and will keep him back. He must be content to be misunderstood, to be misrepresented, but this won't concern him, if he may be hid from men's eyes in the sanctuary of God's presence where his prayers will have power with God.

'I don't put forward this sacred principle of reserve merely in condemnation of others, and their system; what I have said with regard to them is in our defence and for their warning: and we have quite as much need of it for the regulation and protection of ourselves. We are simply advocating great Christian truths which have been forgotten.'

'You are saying that the idea of reserve isn't an innovation introduced by the Oxford Movement?' I said.

'Certainly,' replied Williams. 'In the Scriptures and throughout Church history, Christian teachers, including our Lord, have always been reserved in imparting the gospel. The newcomer to the faith is capable only of receiving "rudiments".

This isn't because he's stupid – he may be very clever. But he needs to grow in grace, and in sensitivity of conscience; then his mind will be able to receive more.

'The whole of the effects which we condemn, and which have developed themselves in a system, amount to a religion which lacks reality, an absence of true seriousness. Of course the principles of the Church are liable to be taken hold of and turned to the same purpose. But I believe that the Church of itself is entirely a system of reserve.

'Actually, the Church holds all the doctrines which those who don't agree with her consider most essential, but in a sort of reserve; being calculated to bring men to the heart and substance of those things of which this scheme embraces the shadow.

'The Church, moreover, in all her ways, is directed to the eye of God, and not to man; as the bride who always looks at the bridegroom, and to no one else. The one aspect of Church practices which is least characterised by reserve is preaching, which she sanctions and admits, and which alone, curiously, this human system has adopted.

'The principle of the Church is that "the secret things belong to the Lord our God" (Deut. 29:29); that He Himself dispenses them through His Church, as He thinks fit, to faith and obedience. Her system therefore is one of reserve.

'The knowledge which Scripture speaks of as life-giving goes entirely with Christian purity of heart; in the scriptural sense, men are still in darkness and ignorance, in proportion to their vices; knowledge is to be imparted or withdrawn on the same principles. God dispenses knowledge of Himself according to man's fitness to receive it.'

Mozley could contain himself no longer.

'Come, come, Williams,' he said, glaring at him. 'Surely we should be working hard to spread the gospel throughout the world!'

'Nothing I've said,' Williams replied firmly, 'limits or confines the most active efforts for propagating the gospel in the world; rather it strengthens these efforts. Our Lord

137

Himself used the very best, the most engaging, and at the same time the most powerful means of recommending truth to men and women. And indeed the Church, in which our Lord has promised to be present to the end, is well compared to His visible body in the flesh. Our Lord reveals Himself according as people will by faith receive Him, will take up the cross after Him, and be His disciples.'

Mozley muttered something which I didn't catch.

'So what's the task of the Church?' I asked.

'The whole business of the Church,' said Williams, 'is to impart to men and women true saving knowledge. In this task, she acts as Jesus did – with reserve; as one who wants above all things to prepare men's minds, and bring them to the truth, but communicating it to them as they are able to receive it. She contains as it were within herself numerous channels or modes of access, by which men may be brought to this knowledge of God.

'The Church's sacramental ordinances – in particular the Lord's Supper – are ways to that invisible Jerusalem, that celestial fellowship, and the city of the living God. The progressive states of proficiency in the school of Christ have been termed the *via purgative*, or the way of repentance; the *via illuminative*, or the way of Christian knowledge; and the *via unitiva*, or the way of charity and union with God.

'Now Church principles contain within them these ways of bringing men to the knowledge of, and to union with God, Who dwells in secret, in a reserved, silent, and retiring way. All those that are considered peculiarly Church principles, doctrines and practices are of this character. For instance, the Church, contrary to the human system which we have described, looks upon houses of divine worship as being especially sacred, and the place of God's peculiar presence. Now if this doctrine of the Church is true, then they must be the home of some great and peculiar blessing; everybody must necessarily agree that God's presence must be life-giving and hallowing, and as it were sacramentally conveying spiritual benefit. These blessings can't be realised except by particular people and attitudes of mind and heart; by those who make it their reverential study to raise their minds to it, and by faith receive the blessing. These privileges, so high and spiritual, are held by the Church in a sort of reserve and silence.

'It's like our Lord in the flesh: conveying now spiritual blessings and then bodily cures in the quiet way without ostentation; and withdrawing Himself from many who might doubt and ridicule these things.

'Bishop Butler showed in his writings that this sense of the holiness of churches is beneficial to the moral character. Jesus overthrew the money changers in the temple.

'The Church is founded on that vast principle in religion that "If any man will do his will, he shall know of the doctrine" (John 7:17 AV). The blessings she promises are all things that depend on the state of the heart: they are real and substantial gifts which have to do with God's unseen presence and are only attained by secret faith and obedience.

'So the Church holds, in a living and substantial way, those great truths of our Lord's divinity and atonement: she holds in secret what others require to be publicly pronounced aloud. Her services contain every doctrine and every principle which has reference to the Holy Spirit: and as members of the Church, by faith and obedience, realise the same, they obtain the blessings of the Spirit.

'Where preaching (or rather eloquence of speech) is too highly regarded, prayer and the sacraments must necessarily lose their value: spirits excited, and moved beyond the tone of God's Word, can't enter in the calm and deep reality of the sacred services.'

'But if the principle of the Church is of such a modest and retiring character,' I asked Williams, 'how can she propagate the gospel far and wide in the world as effectively as the more popular Evangelical system?'

'Well,' said Williams, 'to that it should be a sufficient answer that these are the ways of God – that's what I believe. But I can add that at that early period when the system of reserve was most of all observed in the Church, the gospel spread itself throughout the earth in a way that it's never done since: and all the time they carefully taught that saving truths couldn't be known except by obedience and faith.'

I didn't think that was much of an answer.

'But how can the Church,' I persisted, 'acting under this system of reserve, be such an effective way of extending the faith?'

'Because,' replied Williams, 'all these means we have spoken of as belonging to the Church are ways of obtaining holiness of life and God's favour: and the obedience of Christians is the light of the world; example is the most powerful of persuasions. But besides these, preaching, catechising, and all such means directed to men and women, are most effective when they are based on holiness of life.

'Expediency in things divine is the worst policy: for surely the ways of God are more powerful than those of man. A faithful Church is necessarily a converting Church, for it is of itself "A city on a hill" that "cannot be hidden" (Matt. 5:14). Even when it's silent, in holy reserve it preaches aloud.

'When our Lord in the Sermon on the Mount, after laying down the laws of Evangelical righteousness, proceeded to give directions about the three ways in which His followers could gain power to fulfil His laws (that is, by prayer, giving to the needy and fasting, Matt. 6:1–24), He commanded that they were to be done in secret, with reference alone to our Father, who sees in secret, and will reward openly.

'In these words, Christ spoke (according to the vastness of Divine words) of what must be the essential character of His Church, as therein all duties are by faith to be directed to Him who dwells in secret: and there's something of a reward which is openly promised in this world in that, from the strength thus derived in secret, the example shines before men, who are able to see the good works, and by their own conversion by these means, glorify God.

'And thus, if there are people living in the fear of God, and entirely given up to the things that are unseen, and making great sacrifices to do so, (which has been the purpose with whole bodies of Christians in religious houses) not only by the prevailing power of their prayers, and such means as are known to God only, but as a witness, their efficacy is most powerful in supporting a sense of piety in the world. Such a religion, which has its anchor in the invisible world, isn't moved by the storms of this: a city which has its foundation on the eternal hills, and stands firm like the great mountains.

'In contrast, this modern system, conforming to the character of our own age of expediency, and mostly founded on feeling, is moved by every wind; it shares in the weakness of human things, and can't stand when the floods rise. For surely the system consists, not in sacraments, not in gifts of God given to His chosen, not in divinely appointed ordinances, not in liturgical services, not in prayer, not in obedience, not in the strongholds of the eternal world, and the secret strength of God: but in words and phrases, in professions and emotions, in popular appeals, and party zeal. Very tenderly as I want to speak of individuals that adopt it (some of whom are sincerely attempting to realise the substance of great truths which have been forgotten), yet surely we must see that this religious system has about it something which falls in with, and encourages that spirit of disobedience and lawlessness which is to prevail in the last days.

'The Bible speaks of the Church as a "kingdom of heaven" (Matt. 16:18–19) – it is to be indeed a heaven on earth. And in the progressive attainment of that knowledge "Blessed is the man who fears the Lord, who finds great delight in His commands" (Ps. 112:1).

'The less therefore that these doctrines are received into the heart, the more loudly will they be spoken of: divine fear, like divine love, has ever about it this natural modesty. The true fear of God has little to say, its chief language is that of prayer, and that in secret: as all its ways are directed to One Who sees in secret, it's always afraid of man's praise, and fearless of his reproach.

'Those who most value sacred things will in general say

141

least about them; admiration indeed and joy will find a voice, and a spontaneous expression, as the shepherds spread the word about what they had heard and seen from the angels: but yet in such eloquence there will always be a natural reserve. And even these feelings, when increased greatly and fixed very deeply, will be silent: the shepherds spoke, but Mary was silent, she "treasured up all these things and pondered them in her heart" (Luke 2:19).

'The deep senses and hidden knowledge of Scripture are intended to enlighten and touch our hearts, not to gratify the intellect or try the ingenuity. With regard to any knowledge that is truly valuable, the unhallowed intellect can of itself learn nothing. As in all other matters, in His providence, His moral government, in the events of life, and the thoughts of our minds, God will reveal Himself only to the pure in heart, to the humble and such as keep His commandments. The same is true with regard to His written Word: He will make Himself known to the humble and pure. He will disclose Himself to each in that particular way, perhaps, in which they reverently seek Him; to one in exercises of devotion; to another in acts of love and care; to another in the practice of humiliation; to another in religious fulfilment of practical duties; to another in study of Holy Scripture. Not that either of these can be pursued exclusively to the neglect of the others, for he who breaks one law of his Christian calling is guilty of all.

'The knowledge of Holy Scripture, which is life-giving, may be ever progressive, leading more and more into hidden riches and treasures: the promise is given, and to him who knocks at the door by humble prayer, it will be opened. And he will still have to knock again at the door, and be admitted again into the inner shrine of ever-increasing light; and as he advances onward into better knowledge, and more light, he will see himself more and more deformed and unsightly, until he will wish to be entirely withdrawn from the sight of man, and to be hidden with God.

'Now if we study Scripture with this single eye, under

the guidance of God's Holy Spirit, we shall be preserved and protected by this sacred modesty; it will prevent us from exposing the treasures of God, or His secret gifts; and will suggest to us that so far as we really want to do good to others, we shall observe towards them this forbearance according as they need it. We shall have no need of a system for we shall do it naturally.'

'But isn't the command "Go into all the world and preach the good news to all creation" (Mark 16:15) an unanswerable objection to your whole argument for reserve?' Mozley asked, sounding as if he thought this intervention might cut Williams down to size.

'On the contrary,' Williams replied, 'the question isn't whether we preach the gospel or not, for of course there can be no doubt among Christians about that, but about the most effective method of preaching it. I take it for granted as the first axiom among Christians that the gospel is to be preached. What I have been talking about is the most effective way for Christians to communicate God's truth.

'In John 14:21, it is recorded that Jesus said, "Whoever has my commands and obeys them, he is the one who loves me. He who loves me will be loved by my Father, and I too will love him and show myself to him" and in John 17:6 that He would reveal Himself to His disciples, and not to the world. Now as many don't keep His commands, therefore to many He is not made known. So that to us all, even now our Lord observes this rule of concealing Himself; and therefore all His manifestations in His Church are ways of reserve.

'It's our duty to preach the gospel to the world whether men will hear, or whether they will forbear; we are bound to do it; but it's wise to learn how we may best do it.

'If God does withhold religious truth in a remarkable way, the reason is because such truth is dangerous to us. It's dangerous to us to know it. Therefore the very fact of the atonement, and other great doctrines, being known is an occasion for reverence respecting them.

'Followers of this modern system, who profess to uphold

and value the Bible, set aside the Catholic Church as the interpreter of Scripture, as if it needed none; however it incalculably lowers the reverence for Scripture by making it subject to individual judgment. Although Evangelicals say the Holy Scriptures are divine they treat them as if they weren't; as if human thought could grasp their systems and could limit their meanings.'

I couldn't bring myself to dispute this. I feared there was truth in the allegation.

'If Scripture contains within it the living Word, has a letter that kills, and a Spirit that gives life (2 Cor. 3:6), with far different an attitude ought we to regard it: by prayer, as the Fathers say, we should knock at the door, waiting until He that is within opens to us. The Bible should be approached as that which has a sort of sacramental efficacy about it, and therefore a savour of life, and also unto death; in short, as our Saviour was of old, by them who would acknowledge Him as God, and receive His highest gifts.

'It is of course from a lack of a saving knowledge of God that there exists such a lack of religious fear: for fear can only increase with an increasing knowledge of His presence, and, therefore, with all holiness of life. The subtle and predominant spirit, which is the source of the irreverence of the age, consists in a forgetfulness of God, even in religion, and, therefore, in looking to impression rather than truth. It's seen in a higher regard paid to the pulpit than to the altar. In setting preaching above the sacraments, for that arises from looking to man rather than to God.

'It's not that we're withholding a boon which has been freely given to ourselves; but that with a due sense of its value, God has always associated a reverential modesty in imparting knowledge: for the very nature of Christian knowledge necessarily implies a desire to communicate, while it regulates itself by the laws of true wisdom. Such a desire will always show itself in a forbearance towards the errors of others, allowance for their unavoidable ignorance, and aptitude to teach, arising from watchful endeavours to do them real good.

144

'We may well suppose that the knowledge of Christ can scarcely be better described than by those many descriptions of the pursuit after wisdom, and the way in which she discloses herself to them that seek her. It's the fear of God which is the only access to wisdom.

'All that we know of our Lord's conduct while on earth tells us about our own condition, living in this His dispensation of grace. The meaning of the kingdom of heaven upon earth and the Evangelical revelations consist in this: that God is (as when revealed in the flesh) infinitely near to us, and that if we don't recognise Him, it's our own fault.

'The reserve by which God discloses Himself, in all natural and revealed religion, proves the entrance to His truth to be narrow and confined. It isn't by speculative enquiry, nor learned research, but by deepest humiliation of soul and body, that we must feel after Him, and expect pain and trouble in doing so, knowing that He is a "consuming fire" (Deut. 4:24) and therefore will burn up what is human about us, as we approach Him.

'To know God is entirely a matter of faith, which is to the spiritual life what breath is to the natural life. Our position is rather like that of those who saw our Lord in the flesh. Jesus said, "whoever does the will of my Father in heaven is my brother and sister and mother" (Matt. 12:50). This, and many other similar expressions, imply being brought into some mysterious consciousness of His presence. Obedience itself is quickened and enlivened by Christ's presence, without which, it could not be, and therefore is often called faith or love, as being that in man by which he recognises Him, in opposition to the human understanding.

'Revelation has supplied us through the whole of our moral probation with a living means, a living way, and a living end. The end is personal, and the means also a living Person, our Lord Jesus Christ. The yearnings of our nature after knowledge, the yearnings after love, find their object in Jesus: the friendship and the wisdom, which the heathen philosopher considered as the end and perfection of the practical virtues, and most needed for the soul's rest are here combined – combined in one living object of affection, personal, human and divine.

'All this should encourage us in habits of reverence, reserve, and fear, as considering the awful dispensation under which we walk. We may observe how much there is in this principle to withdraw us from the world, and from the busy excitement that prevails.

'As God has said that He is not in the wind and earthquake, but in the still small voice, so has He shown Himself in all His manifestations to mankind. In the older dispensation He was always as One who, in disclosing, hides Himself. When our Lord appeared on earth in His incarnation, He was still ever as one Who, ever anxious to make Himself known, yet in love for mankind withdrew Himself. The same was always a system of reserve, in which the blessings of the kingdom were laid up, as a treasure hidden in a field (Matt. 13:44).

'The world doesn't know God, and cannot know Him; so far, therefore, as we know Him, so far also the world won't know us, and won't understand our ways and our words. So that from the very nature of the case, this reserve becomes necessary and unavoidable. If we make those secrets of God known to it, we shall injure ourselves, by bringing the gaze of the world into the secrets of God, and His holy place; and injure others also, for those things which they can't understand, they won't reverence.

'If we wish to do good to the world we mustn't look to it, but to God; our strength must be in the secret where God is; the bad instruments of the world mustn't be ours; the platform isn't our strength, no, even the pulpit itself isn't our chief strength; in these we must yield to others if they wish it: but our chief strength must be the altar. Our strength must be in sacraments and prayers, and a good life to give efficacy to them; and in secret giving to the needy. Our strength must be in secret where God is.

'This reserve of Holy Scripture, in which everything that is good must be now more or less concealed, is always calculated to lead on our thoughts to that great manifestation, when there is "nothing hidden that will not be disclosed" (Luke 8:17); neither anything hidden that shall not be known and come abroad, when He who now "sees what is done in secret, will reward you" (Matt. 6:6).'

25   I meet the Regius Professor

'You look troubled,' Mozley said to me.

'I've heard many things in the last twenty-four hours,' I replied. 'Many Bible verses have been quoted which I love. Familiar aspects of Christian truth have been beautifully expressed. Some things have been said which are contrary to what I've always believed. I was just reflecting on it all.'

'Is there anything in particular which perplexes you?' Mozley asked.

'Well, all of you stress your belief in baptismal regeneration. Now, I was baptised as a teenager in a church which taught that baptism only made sense if the candidate was old enough publicly to confess his faith in Christ. Baptism took place subsequent to conversion, which itself was thought to occur when the individual was conscious of having taken a step of faith and commitment to Christ. It all seemed so clear and sensible. Later, when I joined an Evangelical Anglican church, perhaps as many as half the congregation refused to have their children baptised as infants, preferring what they called a "service of dedication".'

Newman looked at Williams and then at Mozley.

'I think he should meet dear Pusey, don't you?'

'I agree,' said Williams. 'Pusey is in any case expecting me at Christ Church.'

'Pusey has written three major tracts on baptism,' said Mozley. 'But don't be misled by the word tract! They're hundreds of pages long and full of footnotes, perhaps the most elaborate treatment of baptism which has appeared in the English language. I don't think Pusey has ever done anything other than thoroughly!'

'You'll like Pusey, I think,' said Newman. 'Of all of us, he's the most warm in his feelings towards those called Evangelicals and the least inclined to be critical of the Reformation.'

Williams, Mozley and I left Newman's rooms in Oriel first. Newman said he'd join us later. As we walked down the High Street towards Carfax, Williams and Mozley told me about Pusey.

'He's Regius Professor of Hebrew and a Canon of Christ Church cathedral,' Mozley began. 'They say he's one of the ablest men at Oxford. When he took his final exams back in 1822, he was examined orally by Keble, who'd taken a double first class degree twelve years earlier. Keble said afterwards that he never knew how Pindar might be put into English until he heard Pusey construe him in his examination. Pindar was a Greek poet,' Mozley added rather breathlessly.

'I remember the senior examiner that year predicting greatness for Pusey,' said Williams. 'He said that he was the man of the greatest ability that he'd ever examined or known. Pusey got a distinguished "first". But I don't think his brilliance is his most remarkable quality – that must be his saintliness. I've no doubt that he has an effect on all the other tractarians. Pusey's presence always checks Newman's lighter and unrestrained moods. I'm always rather silenced by something which I can only describe as "aweful" about him. But there's something congenial about Pusey, an indefinable quality that's absent from Newman and even Keble, both of whom I love dearly.'

We had now reached Carfax and began to walk down St Aldate's.

'Couldn't agree more about Pusey's mixture of saintliness and amiability,' said Mozley. 'But I must tell you a story about Pusey, Newman and Lloyd before we're ushered into the presence. In November 1823, not long after Pusey had graduated, he and Newman joined a small private class run by Dr Charles Lloyd, the Regius Professor of Divinity at Christ Church. Lloyd was an old-fashioned high churchman, a bluff speaker, with a rough, lively, good-natured manner. He would walk up and down the room where he taught taking snuff, and asking his students questions as he went along.

'Lloyd was impatient with the Evangelical views which Newman still held at that time, but apparently liked him personally and respected his abilities. They say that while wandering around his class he would sometimes stop in front of Newman, fix his eyes on him and then pretend to box his ears or kick his shins. But Pusey told me once that he'd never forgotten the course of lectures Lloyd gave them on the Epistle to the Romans. He reckoned that Lloyd taught him not so much the full meaning of the Bible, as how to study it. He never explained more than three or four verses in an hour, but exhausted the history of every doubtful reading, every word and every grammatical construction.'

Just as we reached Christ Church, Newman caught us up. Mozley told me that Pusey's wife, to whom he had been devoted, had died three years earlier. He lived, with his three children, in a house in the south-west corner of Tom Quad which went with the Regius professorship. Apparently the drawing-room looked south over one of the finest views in Oxford.

We walked through the hall and library of the house until we reached the room where Pusey received us. It was large, high, almost square, with two lofty Gothic windows at one of which was a standing desk; there were two or three tables, a sofa, and a number of chairs all weighed down with piles of books. Pusey was sitting in an armed and cushioned chair: he had light curly hair, rounded shoulders and was wearing an academic gown which wasn't buttoned at the elbow, but hung loosely over his wrists.

Pusey looked up at us from under his eyebrows, got up and walked very quickly across the room to greet us. He carried himself like a young man (he would have been forty-two at this time) though he kept his head slightly bowed and looked pale and care-worn. But his expression was as sweet as Williams had described.

Newman spoke first, after the introductions.

'A friend of Bishop Doane has been here wishing to see you,' Newman told Pusey. 'He was in the woods of Transylvania recently with a bedridden old woman. He told her he was going to England, and among other places to Oxford. "Ah," she said, "then you'll see that wicked old man who writes tracts!"'

Pusey laughed.

'I'm sure she meant you,' he said to Newman.

'Mr Steer comes from an Evangelical stable,' said Mozley, 'and is puzzled by some of our views, including on baptism.'

'Ah!' said Pusey. 'Sit down. Soon we shall all have some tea.'

We all sat down.

'When I was a child,' Pusey began, 'I never knew an Evangelical. But over the last twenty-five years I've met many. And ever since I knew them I have loved those who are called Evangelicals. I love them because they love our Lord. I love them for their zeal for souls. I have often thought them narrow; yet I have been drawn to individuals among them more than to others who hold truths in common with myself, which the Evangelicals don't hold, at least explicitly.

'I believe Evangelicals to be "of the truth". I have ever believed and believe, that their faith is, on some points of doctrine, much truer than their words. I believe that they are often withheld from the clear and full sight of the truth by prejudice that that truth, as held by us, is united with error – or that we only indistinctly acknowledge other truths which they themselves hold sacred.

'I have always sought Evangelicals out, both out of love for them, and because I believe that nothing, with God's help, so dispels prejudice as personal discussion, heart to heart, with those against whom that prejudice is held. I sought to point out to them our common basis of faith. I have never met with any Evangelicals who hold the Lutheran doctrine that "justifying faith is that whereby a person believes himself to be justified". To others, who're not Calvinists, I say, "I believe all you believe; we only part where you deny". I have formed lasting friendships with some among them.

'From time to time, as in some of our struggles at Oxford, Evangelicals and I have acted together. I have united with them whenever they would join me in defence of our common faith. Sometimes, when in high places fundamental truths have been denied, I have sought to unite with some who had previously often spoken against me, but against whom I had never spoken.

'I have always felt that common zeal for faith could alone bring together those who are opposed. I have often hoped that, through that common zeal and love, inveterate prejudices which hindered the reception of truth would be dispelled. Whoever teaches any true faith in Jesus is one of God's instruments against unbelief. Such is the power of divine faith, that every child who has it, is such. "From the lips of children and infants you have ordained praise" (Matt. 21:16).

'When our Lord came, the faith of children rebuked the unbelief of the Scribes and the Pharisees. The simple faith of a child has power against unbelief because it's the gift of God. The faith of dissenters, although I think it's often a very naked and fragmentary faith, must in its degree be a power of God against unbelief.

'I tell friends who are dissenters that one thing alone of which the Church of England is jealous: that nothing should seem to overshadow, or interfere with, or supplement the meritoriousness of the one sacrifice of our dear Lord upon the cross. This is what she everywhere guards: "The offering of Christ once made is that perfect redemption, propitiation, and satisfaction, for all the sins of the world, original and actual, and there is none other satisfaction for sin but this alone . . ."

'God blesses through the sacraments; and God blesses through truth. If a Wesleyan minister preaches his simple gospel, that "we are all sinners", that "Christ died to save sinners", that "He bids all sinners come to Him" and says, "whoever comes to me I will never drive away", this is of course fundamental gospel truth, and, when God blesses through it those who know no more, He blesses them through faithful reception of His truth.

'Presbyterians have what they believe; we, what we believe. But those who have observed pious Presbyterians and pious English Catholics, have told me that they discern among our people a spiritual life of a kind which was not among theirs; in a word, a sacramental life. God, the author of truth, has set His seal upon our sacraments. It is in accordance with the truth of the sacraments, that the enlarged life among us has especially taken the form of increased sacraments. The Wesleyan bodies would increase their prayer meetings, which some of them have spoken of to me as their "means of grace". Protestant bodies have their revivals; the Church of England has multiplied the celebration of its sacraments. After more than three centuries, the English Church alone has a more vigorous life than ever. What's the reason? We haven't rejected Catholicism.'

At this point and right on cue, almost as if they sensed from somewhere that their father was beginning to ramble a little, Pusey's children ran into the room. The oldest, a boy called Philip, with curly hair like his father, climbed on to Newman's knee and hugged him. Newman took off his spectacles and put them first on Philip, and then on his little sisters, to peals of laughter.

As Pusey watched, beaming, Newman began to tell the children a story.

'Newman can't bear talking about Church matters all day long,' Mozley whispered to me.

'There was once an old woman,' Newman said to the junior Puseys as they clung on to his knees, 'who had a broomstick. Do you know that this broomstick would go to the well, draw water, and do lots of other things for her? Well, one day the old woman got tired of the broomstick and decided to destroy it. So she cut it in two. Do you know what happened?'

'No, what happened?' chorused Pusey's children.

'To her great dismay,' said Newman, '*two* live broomsticks grew from the broken parts of the old one!'

As the children shrieked with laughter, tea arrived as Pusey had promised. The children were allowed to stay and all talk of serious matters was abandoned for the moment.

26 Giving depth to our Christian experience

After tea, Pusey seemed to remember what Mozley had told him when we were first introduced and began to talk to me about baptism.

'I believe it's largely owing to the absence of the doctrine of baptismal regeneration,' he said, 'that Christian piety among us is often at such a low level. Baptismal regeneration, when connected, as it must be, with the incarnation of our blessed Lord, gives a depth to our Christian experience. It gives an actuality to our union with Christ and a reality to our sonship to God. It gives us an interest in the presence of our Lord's glorified body at God's right hand and a joyousness amid the subduing of the flesh. The doctrine confers dignity on human nature and gives substance to the indwelling of Christ.

'But any careless person may hold baptismal regeneration negatively; the only people who can hold it positively and in its depth are those who have tried to realise it. Sometimes those who hold the doctrine of justification by faith negatively, that is in opposition to the necessity of good works, are accused, rightly, of Antinomianism; but we may just as well make the same accusation against those who abuse the doctrine of baptismal regeneration to lower the greatness of subsequent holiness. Both doctrines may be abused to our destruction.

'Now, I know that those who don't believe in baptismal regeneration usually pride themselves on their respect for the Bible. So let me say straight away that I've no doubt that baptismal regeneration – that God saves us by baptism – is the scriptural doctrine. The plain letter of Scripture says we are saved by baptism (1 Pet. 3:21), and men say, "we are not saved through baptism"; our Lord says, a man must be "born of water and the Spirit" (John 3:5), men that he need not, cannot be born of water; Scripture that we are "saved through the washing of rebirth" (Titus 3:5), man that we are not, and only need to testify to that rebirth; Scripture that "all of you who were baptised into Christ have clothed yourselves with Christ" (Gal. 3:27), man that we have not; Scripture that Christ loved the Church "cleansing her by the washing with water through the word" (Eph. 5:26), man that He did not; Scripture that "we were all baptised by one Spirit into one body" (1 Cor. 12:13), men that we were not but were in that body before.

'The passages of the Bible which refer to baptism, may be divided under two headings: those which directly connect regeneration with it, for example, John 3:5 ". . . no-one can enter the kingdom of God unless he is born of water and the Spirit", and Titus 3:5 ". . . He saved us through the washing of rebirth and renewal by the Holy Spirit"; and those which speak of its privileges, in high indeed and glorious terms, but without the same precision and definiteness.

'There may be a cold and exclusive recognition of the gift of God in baptism, without any vivid perception that that gift can only be retained by abiding faith. In the words "justification by faith" all the Christian privileges and gifts are included, since they are all part of the faith given to one who embraces the mercies of God in Christ, and is through the sacraments made a member of Him. It's justification by God's free grace in the gospel, as opposed to everything outside of the gospel.

154

'It's sad that "justification by faith" came to be mistakenly opposed in men's minds to baptism, the means ordained by Christ Himself for the remission of sin or for justification.

'There are two difficulties in explaining baptismal regeneration: first, it's a mystery; second, men are in these days inclined to lower that mystery. Nicodemus asked "How can this be?" (John 3:9) and most of our questions about baptismal regeneration are Nicodemus' questions. We know it in its author, God; in its instrument, baptism; in its end, salvation, union with Christ, sonship to God, "resurrection from the dead, and the life of the world to come". We only don't know it, where it doesn't concern us to know it: its mode of operation.

'We should love to know how an unconscious infant can be born of God. How can it spiritually live? In what does this spiritual life consist? How can baptism be the same to the infant and to the adult convert? And if it isn't in its visible, and immediate, and tangible effects, how can it be the same at all?

'Yet Scripture makes no difference; the gift is the same, although it varies in its application; to the infant it's the remission of original guilt, to the adult of his actual sins also; but to both by their being made members of Christ, and thereby partakers of His "wisdom . . . righteousness, holiness and redemption" (1 Cor. 1:30); by being made branches of the true vine, and so, as long as they abide in Him, receiving from Him, according to their capacities, and necessities, and willingness, nourishment and life. But if they don't abide in Him, they are thrown away like a branch (John 15:1–8).

'So we can define regeneration as that act whereby God takes us out of our relation to Adam, and makes us actual members of His Son, and so His sons, as being members of His ever-blessed Son; and if sons, then heirs of God through Christ (Gal. 4:7).

'This is our new birth, an actual birth from God, of water, and the Spirit, as we were naturally born of our natural parents. In baptism, too, we are justified, or both accounted and made righteous, since we are members of Him Who is alone righteous. In baptism we are freed from past sin, whether original or actual; have a new principle of life imparted to us, since having been born members of Christ, we have a portion of His life, or of Him Who is our life. In baptism we have also the hope of the resurrection and of immortality, because we have been made partakers of His resurrection, have risen again with Him (Col. 2:9–12).

'The view, then, that we hold of baptism, following the ancient Church and our own, is that we are engrafted into Christ, and thereby receive a principle of life, afterwards to be developed and enlarged by the fuller influxes of His grace.

'Now I heard during tea that you come from Devon,' Pusey said. 'So let me quote from that great master of theology, Richard Hooker, who was born in Heavitree, Exeter.'

'I too was born in Heavitree,' I said, deciding not to mention Hooker's statue in Exeter cathedral close, not knowing whether the statue was there in 1842.

'Well, I'm sure you'll be convinced by a fellow Exonian,' said Pusey, with something of a twinkle in his eye. 'Hooker wrote: "By baptism we receive Christ Jesus, and from Him the saving grace which is proper unto baptism. Baptism is a sacrament which God hath instituted in His Church, to the end that they which receive the same might be incorporated into Christ, and so through His most precious merit obtain as well that saving grace of imputation, which taketh away all former guiltiness, as also that infused divine virtue of the Holy Ghost, which giveth to the powers of the soul the first disposition towards future newness of life."

'Note that whereas regeneration is in Scripture always connected with baptism, there's nothing in Scripture to sever it therefrom. The evidence all goes one way. This, in itself, is very important. For if God, in two places only, assigns the means of His operations, and then in other places were to mention those operations apart from the means, we are not (as some do) to take the texts separately, as if they didn't come from the same giver, but to fill up what isn't expressed in the one by what He teaches plainly in the other.

'So, when we have learnt that the "new birth" or "birth from above" is "of water and the Spirit" (John 3:5) then where it refers to children "born not of natural descent, nor of human decision or a husband's will, but born of God" (John 1:13) we should, with the ancient Church, recognise here also the gift of God in baptism "to all who received him" (John 1:12).

'But not only is there nothing in Scripture to sever regeneration from baptism, but baptism is spoken of as the source of our spiritual birth, as no other cause is, save God: we aren't said to be born again of faith, or love, or prayer, or any other grace which God works in us, but to "be born of water and of the Spirit" in contrast to our birth of the flesh. In order to express that this our new birth of God is, as being of God, a deathless birth, it is described as a birth of seed imperishable, in contrast with our birth after the flesh, of perishable seed through our earthly parents.

'The Bible indeed *connects* other causes besides baptism with the new birth, or rather that one comprehensive cause, the whole dispensation of mercy in the gospel. But no other instrument is ever spoken of in the Bible as having the same relation to our heavenly birth as water. As Christ's merits, and the workings of the Holy Spirit, and faith, and obedience, operate, though in different ways, to the final salvation of our souls, and yet the one doesn't exclude the need for the others, so also the mention of faith, or of the preaching of the gospel, as means towards our regeneration, wouldn't have excluded the necessity of baptism, although mentioned in one passage of Scripture. But now, as if to exclude the idea of human agency in this our spiritual creation, to shut out all human co-operation or boasting, as though we had in any way contributed to our own birth, no loophole has been left to us, no other instrument named; our birth (when its direct means are spoken of) is attributed to the baptism of water and of the Spirit, and to that only.

'These passages alone should lead us to believe that this is the truth about baptism. For although the privileges attached to regeneration are elsewhere spoken of, and the character of mind which conforms to it – our sonship and the mind which we should have as sons, our new creation – yet these are spoken of, as already belonging to, or to be cultivated in us, not as to be begun anew in any one received into the body of Christ. There are tests to discover whether we are acting up to our privilege of regeneration, and cherishing the Spirit therein given us, but there's no hint that regeneration can be obtained in any way except by baptism, or if totally lost, could be restored.

'We are warned that having been saved by baptism through the resurrection of Jesus Christ, we should no longer live for the rest of our time in the flesh to the lusts of men, but to the will of God (1 Pet. 3:21; 4:2), that having been born of imperishable seed, we should rid ourselves of malice, and like new-born babies crave pure spiritual milk (1:23, 2:1–3), that having been saved through the washing of rebirth and renewal by the Holy Spirit, we should devote ourselves to doing what is good (Titus 3:1–8) and again, those who have fallen in any way are exhorted to repentance: but men aren't taught to seek for regeneration or to pray that they may be regenerated. It's nowhere implied that any Christian hasn't been regenerated, or could hereafter be so.

'Our life in Christ is always represented as commencing when we are by baptism made members of Christ and children of God. That life may through our negligence afterwards decay, or be choked, or smothered, or well-nigh extinguished, and by God's mercy again be renewed and refreshed; but a commencement of life in Christ after baptism, a death unto sin and a new birth unto right-eousness, at any other period than at that one first intro-duction into God's covenant, is as unscriptural as a com-mencement of physical life long after our natural birth is impossible.

'Now, we should regard with special reverence any words

which fell from our Saviour's lips, and see that we consider, not what they may mean, but what is their obvious untortured meaning. We shouldn't say with Zwingli, Calvin, Grotius, and the Socinians, that the "water" may be a mere metaphor, a mere emblem of the Spirit; and so, that being "born of water and the Spirit" means nothing more than "being born of the Spirit" without water.

'For Hooker well says, "I hold it for a most infallible rule in expositions of sacred Scripture, that where a literal construction will stand, the farthest from the letter is commonly the worst . . . To hide the general consent of antiquity, agreeing in literal interpretation, they cunningly affirm, that certain have taken those words as meant of material water, when they know that of all the ancients there is not one to be named that ever did otherwise either *expound* or allege the passage than as implying external baptism".

'Not only did the early Fathers of the Church understand the words "water and the Spirit" of baptism, but they regarded them as a sort of key to the rest of Scripture which in any way bore on the same subjects.

'We don't only have the universal consent of the early Church, but we have, in the very earliest writers, an appeal to the then practice, as resting upon the plain meaning of these words of Scripture, and implying an apostolic tradition. The catholicity of this interpretation of our Lord's words, "unless he is born of water and the Spirit" is still further illustrated by the use of them in the baptismal liturgies of the whole ancient Church. There isn't a liturgy, from Britain to India, which doesn't in some way incorporate it.

'Every vestige of Christian writing which God has preserved to us from the ancient Church which explains the words, "unless he is born of water and the Spirit" assumes that they declare that in baptism we are born from above, through our Saviour's gift. Every passage which speaks of the privileges of baptism at all implies the same; their whole system of theology presupposes it; every branch of the whole Church, independent as they may have been in their origin, ingraft upon their baptismal liturgies our Lord's words in John 3:5. The doctrine seems to militate against predestinarian views, yet Augustine, the author of those views, and his disciples, maintained and urged it; until at last, after the Church had borne witness to it for fifteen centuries, one man arose and denied it.'

I remembered reading that Luther always maintained his belief in baptismal regeneration, so I assumed that Pusey was referring to Calvin.

'How can the thought that the long-held belief in baptismal regeneration is an error be consistent with the Saviour's promise never to forsake His Church? But, combining this consent with our Lord's words, the argument becomes so strong that with one who loves his Saviour, and isn't hindered by a long contrary bias, I would gladly rest the whole question of baptismal regeneration upon this one consideration.

'The exposition invented by the Swiss teachers was so manifestly a mere weapon by which to demolish a Papal argument for the absolute necessity of baptism, that it would hardly be worth commenting upon except that no error ever stops at its first stage; mere repetition hardens as well as emboldens.'

So Pusey *was* referring to Calvin.

'Baptism isn't an outward change of state only,' Pusey continued. 'Our Lord declares the mystery, not only of a new birth, but of a birth "from above", "from God", as the beloved disciple from his mouth repeats it, "born of God" (John 1:13).

'No change of heart then, or of the affections, no repentance, however radical, no faith, no life, no love comes up to the idea of this "birth from above"; it takes them all in, and comprehends them all, but itself is more than all; it is not only the creation of a new heart, new affections, new desires, and as it were a new birth, but it's an actual birth from above or from God, a gift coming down from God, and given to faith, through baptism; yet not the work of faith, but the operation of "water and the Holy Spirit", the Holy Spirit giving us a new life, in the fountain opened by Him, even as our Lord was born of Him in the Virgin's womb.

'Faith and repentance are the conditions on which God gives us this new life; water, sanctified by our Lord's baptism, the womb of our new birth; love, good works, increasing faith, renewed affections, heavenly aspirations, conquest over the flesh, its fruits in those who persevere; but it itself is the gift of God, a gift incomprehensible, and not to be confused with or restrained to any of its fruits, (as a change of heart, or conversion) but illimitable and incomprehensible, as that great mystery from which it flows, the incarnation of our Redeemer, the ever-blessed Son of God.

'The words of our Lord "birth from above of water and the Spirit" are a key to Scripture. They are in themselves a high revelation, not to be closed up when we come to read other Scriptures, but flowing into other parts, and imparting to them the light which they contain concentrated within them.

'The Apostle Paul wrote, "But when the kindness and love of God our Saviour appeared, he saved us, not because of righteous things we had done, but because of his mercy. He saved us through the washing of rebirth and renewal by the Holy Spirit, whom he poured out on us generously through Jesus Christ our Saviour" (Titus 3:4–6). The gift moreover is the gift of God in and by baptism; everything but God's free mercy is excluded – "not because of righteous things we had done".

'By faith we are saved, not by works; and by baptism we are saved, not by faith only; we are saved neither by faith only, nor by baptism only; but by faith bringing us to baptism, and by baptism God saves us. They are the words of God Himself.'

'But do you think,' I asked Pusey, 'that all the promises and descriptions of baptism in Scripture apply to infant baptism?'

'Certainly,' Pusey replied, 'unless they did, in effect, infant baptism would be wrong; for so we should be depriving our children of whatever benefits adult baptism conferred, and infant baptism was incapable of. But, since infant baptism is right, then it must confer all the benefits of adult baptism, to be developed thereafter.

'Moreover, where the language of Holy Scripture is unlimited we are not to restrain it. The Bible speaks universally: it says "the washing of rebirth and renewal by the Holy Spirit", "born of water and the Spirit"; how then, are we to say that because our infants are not decayed through actual sin, as were those adults to whom Paul wrote, therefore they are not regenerated and renewed? This would involve the very error of Pelagius, that they needed no renewal, no new birth, having no birth sin.

'The same Scripture pronounces baptism absolutely to be "the washing of rebirth and renewal by the Holy Spirit" and what Scripture calls it, it must remain, at all times, and however applied, to infants as to adults. In all, their Maker's image was defaced; all are renewed after that image in Him, and by being in Him, who is the brightness of His Father's glory and the express image of God.

'These two (John 3:5; Titus 3:4–6) are the only passages of Scripture in which the first origin of regeneration is marked out, and the circumstances under which it takes place are hinted at. And surely this ought, to any careful Christian, to be of great importance; and instead of longing, as some do, for more evidence, he will thank God that the evidence is so clear, that all Christians of old times confidently relied upon it, and transmitted it to us.

'Those who depreciate baptism, appeal to their own inferences from passages in which Holy Scripture isn't speaking of baptism; for example when Paul is speaking of justification; and from these they form a system whereby they depreciate baptism. I have appealed, on the contrary, as the Fathers did, to places where Scripture is speaking of baptism.

'Consider our Saviour's parting words: words on which our very commission to teach, the very security of our existence, depends; words wherein the doctrine of the Holy Trinity is by Him imparted. With these words, and bound up with them the very perpetuity of the Church and the privilege of discipling the nations, is baptism "in the name of the Father, and of the Son, and of the Holy Spirit"; so that thenceforth baptism is the embodiment of our Creed, a living Creed, and the safeguard against every heresy as to the ever-blessed Trinity in Whom we believe.

'Every Church which retains this Creed has the promise of the Saviour of the Church; and should any body of Christians reject this Creed, they cut themselves off from that Church. Baptism in the name of the Holy Trinity, and that saving belief, have been indissolubly linked by our Lord.

'Matthew records the words of the commission given through the apostles to the Church; Mark adds the awful sanction under which it was given. "Whoever believes and is baptised will be saved, but whoever does not believe will be condemned" (Mark 16:16). Through Nicodemus, our Lord warned us that without baptism there could be no entrance into His kingdom; here He tells us that whoever believes in Him will have the blessings which are in Him, imparted to Him, if He is baptised.

'Jesus places two conditions of salvation before us: one required on our part, the other promised on His; one a requisite in us, through His gift in us, the other His gift to us; faith, whereby we desire to be healed, and His gift, whereby He heals us.

'Just as in His bodily miracles Jesus couldn't do many mighty works among his countrymen, because of their unbelief, and He required in them who would be healed faith in Him the Saviour of all, and tells them, "your faith has saved you", yet it wasn't faith alone which healed them, but rather His "virtue" which "went out of Him" and faith was only a necessary condition which, in the fitness of things, He required in those upon whom He should exercise His goodness; so, in this spiritual miracle of our new birth, faith removes the obstacle which sin presents to our receiving the divine instrument.

'Faith turns us to God, who by Adam's fall were turned away from Him; it replaces us in a position of dependence upon Him; it presents us willingly before Him to receive that life which He is and communicates to all His creatures who depend on Him. By one universal law, He has appointed dependence on Him to be a condition of receiving His gifts.

'It's right that we should be careful that our faith is of the right sort; but it's mere egotism, disguised in the form of zeal for purity of faith, which would look upon this as all or as the chief thing. We're not thinking straight if we make that which is required in us the first thing, and God's gift secondary.

'We should never place a quality or qualification in us above that for which it qualifies us; and when our Lord says "he that believes and is baptised will be saved" we shouldn't dissect and sever what He has thus linked together, and hold that we are "saved by faith only" in the sense that baptism is of secondary account, an outward exhibition of what has already taken place inwardly.

'And yet (if they would be honest to themselves) this is the habit of mind of many people, and they regard baptism as of no importance, except as any other act of obedience, having no virtue attached to it, but a sort of encumbrance, which must be taken, and taken thankfully, because it has been recommended, but still is just as much a burden, and as outward, as any rite of the Jewish law was ever held to be – an outward duty to be performed.

'Incidentally, some people suggest that because our Lord, having first limited salvation to those "who believe and are baptised", then adds only that "whoever does not believe will be condemned" would imply that He also would thereby disparage the sacrament, which He had just placed at the threshold and as the very door of salvation. But a very little thought shows that, though our Saviour annexed baptism to belief in Him as a condition of salvation, there was no reason to mention it in the case of unbelief: unbelievers wouldn't be "baptised in Christ's name, for the remission of sins": baptism without faith undoubtedly would save no one. We read in 1 Corinthians 13 that faith without love gains nothing; yet no one would think this was said in disparagement of faith.

'A right understanding of baptism, as the entrance into the kingdom of heaven, is essential to an understanding of the nature of the kingdom of grace, its duties, its comforts, and its privileges. And a correct understanding of one Scripture sets the mind in the right state for God to disclose the meaning of others.'

27   Baptism and sanctification

'In working towards an understanding of baptism,' Pusey said, 'I draw a distinction between "being constrained by the love of Jesus" (the modern emphasis popularised by Evangelicals) and actually receiving power, life from God to change us. Our incarnate Lord imparted to our decayed nature, by His indwelling in it, that principle of life, which through Adam's fall it had lost; and when "through the Spirit of holiness" (Rom. 1:4) which resided in Christ, He raised it from the dead, He made it not only "the first fruits" but the source of our resurrection, by communicating to our nature His own inherent life.

'"I," Jesus says, "am the resurrection and the life" (John 11:25): He not only has obtained, purchased, wills, bestows, is the meritorious cause of, our resurrection; He Himself is it; He doesn't give it us, as it were, from outside, as a possession, as something of our own, but Himself is it to us; He took our flesh, that He might give life to it; He dwelt in it, and obeyed in it, that He might sanctify it; He raised it from death by His quickening Spirit that He might give it immortality: the "first man Adam" was "a living being"; and that life being by sin lost, the last Adam became "a life-giving Spirit" (1 Cor.

15:45). We in His Church, being incorporated into Him, being made members of His body, flesh of His flesh, and bone of His bone, through His sacraments, partake of His life and immortality, because we partake of Him.

'The Apostle Paul wrote, "all of you who were baptised into Christ have clothed yourselves with Christ. There is neither Jew nor Greek, slave nor free, male nor female, for you are all one in Christ Jesus" (Gal. 3:27–8). We see again how the foolishness of God, in what men call carnal ordinances, is wiser than man; and how a false spirituality, by disparaging the outward ordinances, loses sight of the immensity of the inward grace and falls back into legality. By baptism, Christians are truly "in Christ".

'This is how the early Church understood the New Testament epistles; these were the privileges which the early Christians felt they enjoyed: an imparted union with Christ; an actual sonship to God; a partaking of the holiness of Christ, by being partakers of Himself; a separation from the lineage of Adam; a restoration, yes a more than restoration of that bright garment, wherewith Adam was in his innocence invested, stripped whereof he found himself naked; a more than restoration of the image of God, in which man was created, in that He was now recreated in Him, who is "*the* image of the invisible God" (Col. 1:15).

'And for incentives to holiness, or brotherly kindness, or contempt of the world – whether they would persuade men to zeal in keeping themselves holy, in retaining the garment with which they were invested, or to love for those who having, with them, "put on Christ" were also one in Christ, or to despise things transitory when they had things eternal, the truth the first Christians realised gave a spring to high Christian action, which we must now feel to be unstrung. If one member suffered, every other member suffered with it, because they felt themselves to be members of one body, having been baptised into one.

'It wasn't simply that they had been redeemed by the same precious blood, bought by the same price, and had the same hopes, but that they were actually one, being *in* One; and so Christian sympathy vibrated through every member of the whole Church, and what we should scarcely acknowledge as a conclusion of the intellect, they *felt*.

'So far was the vivid sense of this truth from encouraging listlessness (as some now dread) that it was the strongest incentive to vigilance, since the gift was so great, yet might be lost.

'Such was the ancient view: and it's interesting to find that Luther, who retained the ancient doctrine of baptism, clearly understood and taught that the putting on of Christ, which is His gift in baptism, must precede the putting Him on in life; that we must first be by Him conformed to Himself, in order that we may afterwards seek to imitate Him.

'Would those people who extol Luther's clearness on the doctrine of justification by faith, take to heart their master's teaching as to justification through baptism! Luther was a strong, even a polemical, advocate of the doctrine of justification through baptism, and you can read for yourself many extracts from his writings to prove this. It was the Swiss Reformers who were the first to abandon the Church's historic teaching and practice on baptismal regeneration.

'Sadly, the incarnation is now very commonly looked upon in reference only to the passion of our Lord, and as a means of His vicarious suffering; not as if it had any reference to the sanctification of our nature. And so they take what is said of baptism, as teaching only, as if it inculcated the same as circumcision, and imparted a lesson rather than a grace. They only think of the circumcision of the heart which we *ought* to have, of the complete extinction of all sinful tendencies at which we *ought* to aim, of the power of the faith which we *ought* to cherish. Yet this is only a portion of the truth: it tells us of the end which we are to arrive at, but not of the means by which God gives us strength on our way there.

'It's sad but instructive to contrast the poverty of the interpretation of Calvin's school with the richness of that of the ancient Church. There's no doubt that a meagre

167

conception of the actuality of our Redeemer's gifts in His sacraments, whereby He makes men partakers of the divine nature, produced a meagre theology, substituting His teaching for His person, disclosures of God for the mystery of the incarnation.

'Since baptism, as the means of our union with Christ, is the act which conveys to us, either in immediate possession, or as an earnest, all our subsequent blessings, transfers us from being children of wrath, to be children of grace in Him, it could only be that it would often be alluded to by the apostles, writing to Christian churches, even when it wasn't distinctly mentioned; and that the neglect of it must cause much wrong interpretation of the Bible. We must study carefully the whole of Scripture rather than making self-willed selections of passages which we think support our point of view.'

I thought of some friends of mine, Christians for many years, who had recently requested and received believers' baptism. I didn't think there had been anything self-willed about their thinking and subsequent decision to be baptised. They had prayerfully taken this step as a mark of what they believed to be obedience to God and genuine conviction that this was what the Bible taught.

'All the epistles are written to baptised people,' Pusey said. 'So while the fruits of the gifts of baptism, as victory over the world, being temples of the Holy Spirit, are spoken of as present, the gift is uniformly spoken of as past. More than this, the gift is spoken of as having been conferred once and for all (the tense of the verb denotes what has been done once for all) and just as our Saviour's death is spoken of as having taken place once for all, although the fruits of that precious death continue, and shall continue for ever; so also its atoning, justifying, sanctifying influences are spoken of as having been imparted to us through baptism, which took place once for all; though to the faithful they are afterwards continued and enlarged in them.

'And so we have here a remarkable feature of the language

in all the epistles to which men appeal as setting forth *their* notions of justification and "faith". The language is uniform in its principles, and precise and definite in its application. Whenever the justification of individuals is spoken of, it is expressed that justification was bestowed on them in time past, by one act, once for all; it's spoken of as passive on their part, and as complete; "they *were* justified" (Romans 5); and so it isn't said "we are freed from sin", but "Christ freed us", "freed me", "having been made free" (Romans 6); just as Christ said "the truth *will* set you free" (John 8:32).

'To the ancient Church, and those who have followed her teaching, the expressions of the New Testament are just as would be expected. For since baptism is the instrument whereby God communicated to us the remission of sin, justification, holiness, life, communion with the Son and with the Father through the Spirit, the earnest of the Spirit, adoption of sons, inheritance of heaven, all which our Lord obtained for us through His incarnation and precious blood-shedding, it's obvious that all these gifts, and whatever else is included in the gift of being made a "member of Christ" must be spoken of as having been given to Christians, once for all, in *past* time at their baptism. It remains for those who have ceased to regard baptism as the instrument of conferring these blessings to account for the apostle's language.

'Consider Colossians 3:1: "Since, then, you have been raised with Christ, set your hearts on things above, where Christ is seated at the right hand of God." There's no question that Paul refers here to baptism (*see* 2:12). Here (as so often in the epistles) he is beginning to urge upon them a series of Christian duties required of them by their Christian privileges. Scripture knows of no other way whereby we first become partakers of His death than by baptism. It's remarkable that people can see here just a moral exhortation to conformity to Christ, without any allusion to the hidden spring of such action, our union with Him and the power of His resurrection derived into us from Him through the fount of baptism.

'In Ephesians 4:4–6, we read, "There is one body and one Spirit – just as you were called to one hope when you were called – one Lord, one faith, one baptism; one God and Father of all, who is over all and through all and in all." It's not then as an outward form that baptism is here named, but as "in power" sealing us, and sealing up our faith in us, which in it was named upon us, and in which we were baptised, our faith in the Father, Son and the Holy Spirit. Where moderns see only a general argument for what they think is Christian unity, a unity of will, the ancients saw actual union through "the one baptism in the one faith, in one Lord and one God".

'1 Corinthians 12:12–13 says, "The body is a unit, though it is made up of many parts; and though all its parts are many, they form one body. So it is with Christ. For we were all baptised by one Spirit into one body – whether Jews or Greeks, slave or free – and we were all given the one Spirit to drink." To be baptised into Christ is to be baptised in the one Spirit; and neither is the baptism of Christ without the Spirit, nor is there a baptism of the Spirit without the baptism instituted by Christ. This identity of illustration more closely identifies the baptism into Christ with the baptism in the Spirit. For in baptism the Spirit is the agent. There's no distinction, as if some were baptised into the "outward body of professing believers", as it is sometimes put, others into the invisible body of Christ, the true Church; or that some were baptised with water, others with the Spirit.

'In Acts, baptism isn't urged on converts as a proof of sincerity, or a test of faith, but for its own benefits. In Acts 2 we read that when Peter finished his sermon on the Day of Pentecost, the people were cut to the heart and said to the apostles, "'Brothers, what shall we do?' Peter replied, 'Repent and be baptised, every one of you, in the name of Jesus Christ for the forgiveness of your sins. And you will receive the gift of the Holy Spirit'" (Acts 2:37–8). We read that the disciples fulfilled their Lord's command, that it was by baptism that they enlarged their

Lord's Church; that it was by baptism that men were saved.

'A few verses later we read, "Those who accepted his message were baptised, and about three thousand were added to their number that day" (Acts 2:41). This continues to be the marked character of the Acts throughout, so that (with the exception of Sergius Paulus) there isn't one account of any remarkable conversion, in which it isn't expressly stated also that the individual so converted was baptised.'

28 Unanswered question

'I remember reading that disciples of the Oxford Movement are sometimes known as Puseyites,' I said. 'How would you summarise what a Puseyite believes?'

'Well, of course, it horrifies me when I hear the term. Just as I can't imagine that anyone would prefer to be thought of as a Calvinist, a Lutheran or a Wesleyan than a Christian, so I hope no one would wish to be known as a Puseyite – quite apart from its ugly sound! But I accept that I'm associated, together with Newman, Keble, Williams and others, with a recognisable movement.

'Simply stated, we have aimed to assert the divine origin of the Church and to work for its renewal in the face of growing secularism and rationalism. Let me begin to answer your question by listing six things which summarise our way of thinking.

'First, we have high thoughts on the two sacraments of baptism and the Lord's Supper; second, a high estimate of episcopacy as God's ordinance; third, a high estimate of the visible Church as the body in which we are made and continue to be members of Christ; fourth, we have a high regard for ordinances, as directing our devotions and disciplining us, such as daily public prayers, fasts, feasts and so on; fifth, we have regard for the visible part of devotion, such as decoration

171

of the house of God, which acts insensibly on the mind; and sixth, reverence for and deference to the ancient Church, of which we see the Anglican Church as the representative to us, and by whose views and doctrines we interpret our own Church when her meaning is questioned or doubtful: in a word, reference to the ancient Church, instead of our Reformers, as the ultimate expounder of the meaning of our Church.

'But these six points are matters of degree only. In addition, there is a broad line of difference between the views of the Oxford Movement and the system of Calvin (which has been partially adopted in the Anglican Church). The main points are:

'First, what are the essential doctrines of saving faith? We say, those contained in the Creeds, especially what relates to the Holy Trinity. The other (Calvinist), the belief in justification by faith only.

'Second, belief in a universal judgment of both good and bad according to their works.

'Third, the necessity of continued repentance for past sins.

'Fourth, the intrinsic acceptableness of good works, especially of deeds of charity (sprinkled with the blood of Christ), as acceptable through Him for the blotting out of past sins.

'Fifth, the means whereby a man, having been justified, remains so. The one (the Calvinist) would say, by renouncing his own works and trusting to Christ alone; the other, by striving to keep God's commandments through the grace of Christ, trusting to Him for strength to do what is pleasing to God, and for pardon for what is displeasing, and these bestowed especially through the Lord's Supper as that which chiefly unites us with our Lord.

'Sixth, the sacraments regarded in the Calvinistic system as signs of grace given independently of them; by the Anglican Church as the very means by which we are incorporated into Christ, and subsequently have this life sustained in us.

'Seventh, the authority of the universal Church as the channel of truth to us. The Anglican Church thinks that what the universal Church has declared to be a matter of faith (as the Creeds) is to be received by individuals, independently of what they themselves see to be true. The other that a person is bound to receive nothing but what he himself sees to be contained in the Holy Scriptures.'

Then Pusey said something which surprised me, after all I'd heard.

'I am, however, more and more convinced,' he said, 'that there's less difference between right-minded people on both sides than they often suppose – that differences which seemed considerable are really so only in the *way of stating them*; that people who express themselves very differently, and think each other's mode of expressing themselves very faulty, mean the same *truths* but express them differently.'

'Well, I certainly find your last remark comforting,' I said. 'But, on the question of the pursuit of holiness, which all of you have stressed – I gather that you think Evangelicals fall short in this area?'

'Well, we all readily admit that many Evangelicals live truly godly and devoted lives,' said Pusey. 'But we do think there's a flaw in their teaching on holiness.'

'So what's the flaw?' I asked.

'Evangelicals often seem to me,' said Pusey, 'to carry their ideas of corrupt human nature too much into the new man. They think that, because we are by nature infected with evil, and have ourselves gone yet further astray, therefore we are incapable of rising to any great heights of holiness (though this is always God's free gift, and not of ourselves). Evangelicals almost seem to look upon it as derogatory to Christ's atonement, if we are thought of as anything other than weak, miserable, sinning creatures, who are to go on sinning and polluted unto our lives' end. They forget that since it's not ourselves but God Who makes us holy, all boasting and self-righteousness is excluded by the very conditions. I suspect that there lies, unknown to these

173

good people, a stronger idea of human agency than they themselves are aware of, that they depreciate human actions because they think too much of it as human.

'However I must say, since you've asked me, that the result is a miserably low standard of human attainment among Evangelicals. Or, to put it another way, a lack of faith, as to what God can and has and does work in us for our redemption, or of Christ's being at the right hand of God to make intercession for us. They don't think of that almost more stupendous mystery, man united with God, our human nature (which has not been vouchsafed to angels) united with our God, and all the high inconceivable privileges ensuing from that.'

'How strong,' I asked Pusey, changing the subject a little, 'do you think Evangelicalism will be in a hundred and fifty years' time? Or do you think the Church will by then be entirely Catholic in its thinking?'

As I asked this, the door opened and Pusey's three children ran in, dressed in their night clothes. This time, though, they didn't run to Newman; they hurled themselves at me. Philip, the oldest, began to pull my hair while his sisters set about vigorously poking me in the ribs.

'Stop it!' I yelled. 'That hurts!'

Strangely, I felt unable to move or fend off my attackers. Then I felt a hand on my shoulder.

'Would you mind, Sir? This is a place of worship and prayer, as well as a tourist attraction.'

The speaker was one of St Mary's vergers. Behind him stood two Japanese visitors with expensive cameras admiring the pulpit from which Newman had preached a hundred and fifty years earlier.

'I'm so sorry,' I said. 'I must have dozed off. I had the most incredibly vivid dream . . .'

The verger wandered off.

I would never hear a reply to my question to Pusey and would have to answer it myself. The dream remained with me as a vivid reality. Outside in the streets of Oxford again,

174

in warm sunshine, I thought of the criticisms I had heard of Evangelicals.

According to the men I had met in my dream, Evangelicals were obsessed with a slogan 'justification by faith', brought to prominence in the stormy years of the Reformation; this alleged obsession had distorted their thinking and dominated their presuppositions. Claiming to make the Bible the ultimate authority in their faith, Evangelicals had been accused of using selected passages – especially parts of Paul's epistles – to support their version of the faith. They were found guilty of paying too little attention to passages like the Sermon on the Mount, with its high standard of Christian righteousness and absence of obvious references to the atonement.

Newman had complained that Evangelicals had lost the simplicity and unworldliness of writers like Joseph Milner and Thomas Scott whom he had so much enjoyed as a young man. Now their writers and preachers played into the hands of liberals so that the Evangelical religion wasn't well equipped in the battle against rationalism.

Ward had argued vigorously that the Lutheran principle of justification by faith destroyed the whole idea of self-conquest. It involved a total passivity so that the average standard of saintliness and the normal level of Christian attainment was miserably low. Evangelical religion denied the first principles of morality, and too often had become a religion of feeling rather than duties. Agnostics might legitimately complain that popular religion aimed at salvation rather than morality.

The inevitable result, these men told me, of a simplistic belief in justification by faith was that it led to a religion of emotion. In his most forthright criticism, Ward had argued that to the extent that the modern Evangelical system denied that obedience to God and the dread of sin were essential and necessary truths, and counted it the chief glory of the gospel that under it they were no longer truths, then a religious heathen adopting the Evangelical faith would be exchanging the fundamental truth of the world of nature

175

and the demands of conscience (Rom. 1:19–20; 2:14–15) for fundamental error. Lutheranism contradicted truths which were first principles: conscience is supreme in the pursuit of moral and religious truth.

According to the men of the Oxford Movement, Luther had found Christians in bondage to their works; he released them by his doctrine of faith, and left them in bondage to their feelings. The Evangelical system puts knowledge first and obedience afterwards. Whereas Scripture always introduces the warning clause 'if you keep the commandments', Evangelicals tend to say 'if you don't think of them too much'.

Evangelical teaching which led people to think that good works were of minor importance, and spoke slightingly of them, that is works of charity, of humiliation, and prayer, taught men false and dangerous doctrine. This teaching flattered human indolence, but opposed Scripture, opposed the Church and opposed the first principle of our moral nature.

According to Williams, the Evangelical system unduly exalted preaching to the detriment of an emphasis on obedience as the best means of promoting Christianity in the world. The system tended to exclude everything that might alarm the consciences of its followers, obedience to Church authority, practices of mortification, the fear of God, and the doctrine of judgment to come. It set out religion in colours attractive to the world, by stimulating the affections, and by stifling the conscience, rather than by purifying and humbling the heart.

Instead of the process of painful self-discipline and gradual restoration, or the system of penance of the ancient Church, Evangelical Christianity offered an instant route to arriving at the privileges and authority of advanced piety. The result was that real humility of heart, and a quiet walking in the ordinance of God, found not only the world in array against it, but Christianity also. And the system was marked by a lack of reverence. The Evangelical religion, they told me, took all that was agreeable and beautiful and benevolent in

176

Christianity, and rejected what was stern and self-denying and awful.

In contrast to all this, I recalled the recurring strands of positive thought which ran through so much of what Newman, Ward, Williams and Pusey had said. They had stressed the importance of conscience as the voice of God within – the importance of the sense of duty: 'thou shalt' whispering within us and even within the pagan heart. How *obedience* must come first, then knowledge – that obedience was the air in which religious faith lived. It was, as Jesus told us, the pure in heart who see God.

The Church, they told me, should insist on the intrinsic worth of moral effort and recognise that religion should develop from and not contradict the natural religion of which Paul speaks in the second chapter of Romans.

An important function of the Church was to 'train up saints'; ascetic discipline was needed to raise the moral tone. And so the Church needed to use these methods: meditation; examination of conscience; retreats; the literature of ascetic theology and the lives of saints; the confessional; and moral theology. Although good works can't be done except through the grace of God, there must be careful moral discipline as the foundation on which to build Christian faith.

Sin was the great enemy to be feared not self-righteousness; obedience to the will of God was the one thing most needed. Love was the discriminating mark and moulding principle under which mere belief (which demons exercise) was converted into faith and made justifying: faith wasn't justifying unless informed and animated by love. This, they said, was the historic Christian faith even though, in his day, Luther had vehemently denied it.

Justification, they had told me, comes *through* the sacraments; is received *by* faith; consists in God's inward presence; and *lives* in obedience. Justification is a real and actual communication to our souls of the atonement through the work of the Spirit: the dwelling in us of God the Father and the Lord incarnate through the Holy Spirit. To be justified is to receive God's very presence within us, and be made a temple of the Holy spirit. 'Christ in us' – that, Newman had told me, is our justification.

Preachers should take care to encourage congregations to make sure their faith is justifying, that it isn't dead, formal, self-righteous, or merely moral instead of glorifying Him, Whose image fully set out, destroys deadness, formality and self-righteousness.

Religious doctrines and articles of faith can only be received in a certain state of heart; this state of heart can only be formed by a repetition of certain actions. The obedience of Christians was the light of the world; example was the most powerful of persuasions. God would reveal Himself to the pure in heart, to the humble, and those who, in His strength, kept His commandments. The fear of God was the only access to wisdom. By faith, I was told, we are saved, not by works; and by baptism we are saved, not by faith only; we are saved neither by faith only, nor by baptism only; but by faith bringing us to baptism, and by baptism God saves us.

All the views of the men of the Oxford Movement, which I have recorded as a dream, are of course based on their own writings. Even the little incidents I have recounted are mostly based on actual events described by contemporaries.

To what extent were the Oxford Movement's criticisms of popular Christianity still true? – I wondered. Hadn't John Stott, the great Evangelical preacher and writer of the twentieth century, preached on the Sermon on the Mount at the Keswick Convention? I had with me his book *The Message of the Sermon on the Mount*.

'I think,' Stott writes in his preface, 'we should value tradition more highly than we often do, and sit more humbly at the feet of the masters.' I noticed that his sources included two early Christian Fathers, Augustine and Chrysostom, as well as Calvin and Luther. Further on in his preface, Stott says, 'Jesus did not give us an academic treatise calculated

178

merely to stimulate the mind. I believe He meant His Sermon on the Mount to be obeyed.'

I felt sure that all the men I had met in my dream would have approved of Stott's argument that the essential theme of the Bible from beginning to end was that God's historical purpose was to call out a people for Himself; that is a holy people, set apart from the world to belong to Him and to obey Him; and that its vocation is to be true to its identity, that is, to be holy or different in all its outlook and behaviour.

I saw that Stott argued that the Sermon on the Mount portrayed the repentance (*metanoia*, the complete change of mind) and the righteousness which belong to the kingdom of heaven. On the Christian's relationship to the law, Stott writes that,

> Jesus had not come to abolish the law and the prophets, He said, but to fulfil them. He went on to state both that great-ness in God's kingdom was determined by conformity to their moral teaching, and even that entry into the kingdom was impossible without a righteousness greater than that of the scribes and Pharisees (Matt. 5:17–20) . . . The ultimate issue posed by the whole Sermon concerns the authority of the preacher. It is not enough either to call Him 'Lord' (7:21–23) or to listen to His teaching (7:24–27). The basic question is whether we *mean* what we say and *do* what we hear. On this question hangs our eternal destiny [no crude notion of justification by faith here!]. Only the man who obeys Christ as Lord is wise. For only he is building his house on a foundation of rock, which the storms neither of adversity nor of judgment will be able to undermine . . .
> I fear that we Evangelical Christians, by making much of grace, sometimes thereby make light of sin. There is not enough sorrow for sin among us.

And, in a section commenting on Matthew 5:19–20, Stott writes,

179

Christian righteousness is greater than pharisaic righteousness because it is deeper, being a righteousness of the heart. Pharisees were content with an external and formal obedience, a rigid conformity to the letter of the law; Jesus teaches us that God's demands are far more radical than this. The righteousness which is pleasing to him is an inward righteousness of mind and motive. For 'the Lord looks at the heart' (1 Sam. 16:7) . . . We must not imagine (as some do today) that when we have the Spirit we can dispense with the law, for what the Spirit does in our hearts is, precisely, to write God's law there. So 'Spirit', 'law', 'righteousness' and 'heart' all belong together . . . What Jesus is contradicting is not the law itself, but certain perversions of the law of which the scribes and Pharisees were guilty. Far from contradicting the law, Jesus endorses it, insists on its authority and supplies its true interpretation (p. 76).

As I put Stott's book down, I thought that there was much here of which the men of the movement would approve. But how typical was his thinking of the Evangelical world generally?

29 Waking up

Evangelicalism is growing in strength in Britain and many parts of the world. Evangelical Christianity has much to commend it: it can fill churches, attracting young people and families as well as the older generation. Its worship, often with a strong Charismatic influence, is vibrant, joyfully alive, contemporary in style and Christ-centred. It encourages earnest habits of prayer and Bible study and demonstrates a genuine desire to reach out to the community at home and abroad, not only with the message of salvation, but also with practical expressions of the love of Christ. Numerous social projects working in deprived areas, and the work of caring agencies such as Tear Fund, are a testimony to a brand of Christianity which is far more than nominal.

However, it has seemed to me that the portraits of the Evangelical scene drawn by Mozley, Ward, Newman and Williams stand as accurate descriptions of some parts of that world today. Evangelical Christianity is, I think, still permeated by a tendency towards Antinomianism. We so stress that salvation is all of God's grace, that good works and a rigorous pursuit of a self-denying holiness are too often seen, not simply as unnecessary, but even as rather distasteful. You do still hear sermons like the one Newman referred to in Chapter 17 above. Is this the tendency the Archbishop of Canterbury, Dr George Carey, had in mind when he was recently quoted as saying that 'while Evangelicals are in the business of making people Christians, Catholics are in the business of making them holy'?

Why is it that some strands of Evangelical thinking and practice remain very much like those identified by the men of the Oxford Movement over a hundred and fifty years ago? No doubt there are some Evangelicals – but I suspect very few – who are aware of the movement's strictures about them and have rejected the criticisms as invalid or theologically unsound. A far greater number, I believe, don't realise that a reasoned, Biblical and spiritual case can be made against some of the leading assumptions of Evangelical Christianity. This case was put vigorously and articulately by the men of the movement taking their stand on a vision of the universal Church as a great historical reality; the same case has also been put independently over the last two hundred years by theologians in other countries including Denmark and Germany.[1] It is a case which, its advocates claim, is not only biblical but magnifies the grace of God and fully understands the wonder of the atonement – even if it is held that this doctrine is best promoted after people's minds have been prepared so that they are best able to receive it.

181

I have certainly come across confusion and disagreement amongst Evangelicals over the relationship of the Christian to God's moral law – few see this as clearly and cogently as, for example, John Stott and Sir Norman Anderson.[2] In theory and in practice this seems often to be an area of muddle.

And, historically, isn't it true that the Reformation idea that each Christian is encouraged to interpret Scripture as he or she thinks right, or as they believe God is guiding them, independently of the teaching of the historic Christian Church, has in practice resulted in splits, divisions, hatred, a multiplication of sects, fanaticism and even bloodshed?

Is it too much to hope that, in these days when authoritarian and hierarchical structures are even less warmly regarded than in the nineteenth century, a return to a high view of the Church might be seen as a part of God's will for the future? Christians who love the historical form of the Church, its liturgical worship, agelessness, and embodiment of eternal truth do not regard 'tradition' as a dead, formal, unspiritual affair but as the vigorous life of the Holy Spirit in the Christian community over the centuries – illuminating, as the Spirit of Truth, the Church's teaching and guiding, as Counsellor, her practice.

Of course, thinking on the role and definition of 'the Church' has developed since the days of the Oxford Movement. But one strand in the thought of the tractarians is particularly fashionable at the end of the twentieth century. Isaac Williams emphasised that the Bible speaks of the Church as a 'kingdom of heaven'. He quoted our Lord's words to Peter, 'on this rock I will build my church, and the gates of Hades will not overcome it. I will give you the keys of the kingdom of heaven . . .' (Matt. 16:18–19). Williams argued that the Church is to be a heaven on earth (*see* Chapter 24 above).

In line with this, Roger Beckwith and Martin Dudley have pointed out recently that 'what Christ proclaimed was, not the Church, but the "reign" or "kingship" or "kingdom" of God. In the same way, as the community that has Christ as its foundation and that lives "in Christ" and is both sign and instrument of His saving work the Church proclaims the kingdom of God'.[3] Beckwith and Dudley go on to quote from the first Report of the Inter-Anglican Theological and Doctrinal Commission, 'The Church . . . is engaged in the same business as its Lord: that of opening the world to its horizon, to its destiny as God's kingdom. Not only by proclamation but also by deed, the Church is called to let God's kingdom show in the world and for the world – to give the world a taste, an inkling, of "the glory which shall be revealed"'.[4]

Archbishop Michael Ramsey has reminded us that the Church isn't a static institution. 'To be "Church",' he wrote, 'is always turning to God, always to be in transition to a better mind, always to be answering afresh the call of God in Christ as events and circumstances make that call concrete.'[5]

So where do I go from here?

Today, I returned to the little village in Devon where I live with my family. We are happy members of the only place of worship in the village, a Methodist Church. Still today, candidates wanting to become Methodist local preachers have to satisfy the examiners that they have studied selected sermons of John Wesley.

How would Wesley have reacted to the views of the men of the movement which began in his own university forty years after his death? Wesley, himself the son of a high church clergyman, repeatedly emphasised that he had introduced no new doctrines into the Christian religion. 'Why, these are only the common fundamental principles of Christianity!' he wrote of his views in his *Character of a Methodist*.

On the fundamental doctrine of justification, Newman and Wesley appear to have been surprisingly close. Justification by faith was certainly a fundamental strand in Wesley's teaching; but the doctrine never led him into the trap of Antinomianism. 'If he was at all inclined to this,' writes J. H. Overton in his study of Wesley, 'when the Moravian influence was yet fresh, he very soon corrected himself. "I fell," Wesley says, "among some Lutheran and Calvinist authors, whose confused and undigested accounts magnified faith to such an amazing size, that it quite hid all the rest of the commandments." This would never suit the practical mind of John Wesley. Nor did this doctrine of justification by faith at all lead him to make light of the necessity of repentance. "Repentance absolutely must go before faith; fruits meet for it, if there be opportunity." Justifying faith cannot exist without previous repentance. "Whoever desires to find favour with God should cease to do evil, and learn to do well."

'In fact,' Overton continues, 'no one who reads John Wesley's works candidly and intelligently can for a moment charge him with exalting faith to the disparagement of those good works which are its inseparable results. John Wesley was a true preacher of righteousness; and the most violent opposition he ever aroused was on the score of laying too much stress upon good works. Faith and holiness, justification and sanctification, were separable in thought, but quite inseparable in fact . . .

'It must,' writes Overton, 'be clearly explained that by faith Wesley meant far more than belief. It was at least as much a moral and spiritual and intellectual act. "What," Wesley asks, "is faith? Not an opinion nor any number of opinions, be they ever so true. A string of opinions is no more Christian faith than a string of beads is Christian holiness."'

In November, 1760, Wesley wrote, in a letter to the Editor of *Lloyd's Evening Post*, that

> the fundamental doctrine of the people called 'Methodists' is, Whosoever will be saved, before all things it is necessary that he hold the true faith; the faith which works by love; which by means of the love of God and our neighbour, produces both inward and outward holiness. This faith is an evidence of things not seen; and he that thus believes is regenerate, or born of God; and he has the witness in himself (call it assurance, or what you please); the Spirit

184

Himself beareth witness with his spirit that he is a child of God. This is 'The true portraiture of Methodism' so-called. 'A religion superior to this' (the love of God and man), none can 'enjoy', either in time or in eternity.

Wesley was sparing in his use of the word conversion, because he said it didn't often occur in the New Testament; and he also seems to have preferred the term new birth to conversion, because the former implied the idea of pain, travail, effort; in a word, repentance, on which, as a practical man, Wesley laid great stress.

If Wesley and the leaders of the Oxford Movement would have agreed on justification, we can say, perhaps to the surprise of many, that they were also close in their approach to the sacraments.

All through his life, Wesley attached great importance to the sacraments, and the way in which he dealt with them shows how unaltered his views were from his youth in a high church rectory to old age. An extract from his *Treatise on Baptism*, which he published in 1756, nearly twenty years after his Aldersgate experience, shows that Pusey would have heartily approved of Wesley's view of baptismal regeneration:

By baptism we, who were 'by nature children of wrath' are made children of God. And this regeneration, which our Church in so many places ascribes to baptism, is more than barely being admitted into the Church, though commonly connected therewith; being 'grafted into the body of Christ's Church, we are made the children of God by adoption and grace'. This is grounded on the plain words of our Lord, 'Except a man be born again of water and of the Spirit, he cannot enter the kingdom of God'. By water, then, as a means, the water of baptism, we are regenerated or born again. Herein a principle of grace is infused, which will not be wholly taken away, unless we quench the Holy Spirit of God by long-continued wickedness.

But surely Wesley didn't believe in baptismal regeneration when he preached the necessity of new birth to those who had already been baptised? That he certainly did believe this is clear from his famous sermon on the new birth.

It is certain our Church supposes, that all who are baptised in their infancy are, at the same time born again; and it is allowed, that the whole office of the baptism of infants proceeds upon this supposition. Nor is it an objection of any weight against this, that we cannot comprehend how this work can be wrought in infants. For neither can we comprehend how it is wrought in a person of riper years . . .

The beginning of that vast, inward change is usually termed the new birth. Baptism is the outward sign of this inward grace, which is supposed by our Church to be given with and through that sign to all infants, and to those of riper years, if they repent and believe the gospel. But how entirely idle are the common disputes on this head! I tell a sinner, 'You must be born again!' 'No,' say you, 'he was born again in baptism; therefore he cannot be born again.' Alas, what trifling is this! What, if he was *then* a child of God? He is *now* manifestly a child of the devil; for the works of his father he doeth. Therefore do not play upon words. He must go through an entire change of heart. In one not yet baptised, you would yourself call that change the new birth. In him, call it what you will; but remember meantime that if either he or you die without it, your baptism will be so far from profiting you that it will greatly increase your damnation.

A few sentences from a sermon by John Wesley on the Lord's Supper, published in 1788, will illustrate his teaching on this sacrament. Having spoken of it as 'the food of our souls', which 'gives strength to perform our duty, and leads us on to perfection', he goes on, let every one, therefore, who has either any desire to please God, or any love of his own soul, obey God, and consult the good of his own soul, by communicating every time he can; like the first Christians, with whom the Christian sacrifice was a constant part of the Lord's service. And for several centuries they received it every day; four times a week always, and every saint's day beside. Accordingly, those that joined in the prayers of the faithful never failed to partake of the blessed sacrament.

In spite of strong and persistent pressure, he refused to allow his lay preachers to administer either the sacrament of baptism or the Lord's Supper – and this continues to be Methodist practice today.

Two years before he died, in his famous sermon 'On the Ministerial Office', Wesley wrote,

The Methodists are not a sect or party; they do not separate from the religious community to which they at first belonged; they are still members of the Church; such they desire to live and die. And I believe, one reason why God is pleased to continue my life so long is to confirm them in their present purpose, not to separate from the Church.

Also like the leaders of the Oxford Movement, Wesley didn't accept Calvin's doctrine of the final perseverance of the saints ('once saved always saved'). He did however, as is well known, teach a doctrine of assurance. This was simply the assurance of present pardon, and might be, and very often was, lost. The Christian, he wrote, 'has the witness in himself (call it assurance, or what you please); the Spirit Himself beareth witness with his spirit that he is the child of God'. And so the Catechism currently used by Methodists states that 'All need to be saved; all may be saved; all may know themselves saved; all may be saved to the uttermost.' But due to sin, this sense of assurance may be lost.

Thus it appears from Wesley's own writings and published sermons that his teaching had much in common with that of the Oxford Movement. What he would have thought of their doctrine of reserve I'm not sure. But it's interesting that perhaps the most energetic evangelist England has ever seen, who travelled an estimated two hundred and fifty thousand miles on horseback to preach the gospel, was an enthusiastic advocate of the doctrine of baptismal regeneration.

So, if I were to accept the views of Newman, Ward, Williams and Pusey as including valuable insights for today, useful warnings against distortions in Evangelical thinking, it seems that I should be able to hold my head high in a Methodist pulpit – though I'm bound to say that the ethos of many parts of current Methodism, owe more to a combination of Billy Graham, the charismatic movement and Graham Kendrick, than to John and Charles Wesley.

30 The beauty of holiness

It has been difficult fully to convey the *tone* of the Oxford Movement, and the reputation for saintliness which its leaders earned.

The movement came to discourage anything which was showy; it came to stress the exercise of an inner and unseen self-discipline and the cultivation of what Dean Church called 'the less interesting virtues of industry, humility, self-distrust and obedience . . . It was from the first a movement from which, as much by instinct and temper as by deliberate intention, self-seeking in all its forms was excluded. Those whom it influenced looked not for great things for themselves, nor thought of making a mark in the world'.

The note Newman struck in the first of his published sermons – 'Holiness necessary for future blessedness' – was never lost. Seriousness, reverence, the fear of insincere words and unsound professions, were essential in the character which was expected in those who made common cause with the movement.

The leaders of the movement encouraged a training in Christian discipleship which issued often in a steady and unconscious elevation of the Christian character. How this character was fed, nurtured, encouraged and warned of its dangers may be seen at its best in the published sermons of Newman, Pusey and Keble – and of course in the movement's poetry and hymnody, some of which is enjoyed and sung today as much by Evangelicals as high churchmen.

> Sun of my soul, Thou Saviour dear,
> It is not night if Thou be near;
> O may no earth-born cloud arise
> To hide Thee from thy servant's eyes.
>
> (John Keble)

Even those who ultimately left the movement for various reasons retained its moral stamp, its value for sincerity and simplicity of feeling and life, and a keen sense of the awefulness of things unseen.

In assessing the theological soundness and intellectual rigour of the Oxford Movement's teaching, it's worthwhile to remember that you couldn't be accepted for a course of study leading to a degree at Oxford at that time unless you subscribed to the Thirty-nine Articles of the Church of England; nearly all the dons were clergymen, and all except the heads of houses (masters of colleges and 'halls') and some professors were celibate.

Most people would have agreed with Tom Mozley that Oxford was the most important theological university in the world – the only rival to the Vatican in terms of status and scholarship. Few Christian writers have surpassed the writings of Newman and Pusey for thoroughness and, in Newman's case, for elegance and originality of expression.

Just as the movement was marked by a high moral tone,

189

it was also, I believe, Christ-centred. We have heard Pusey say that he loved the Evangelicals because of their zeal for souls. His own zeal for souls was seen in his support for missionary work, church planting, personal counselling and in his preaching. He had none of Newman's silver intonation, preaching rather in a low, deep, rather monotonous voice, which, in his later years, became husky and thick. But there were passages of unstudied eloquence, with an almost mystical quality; and passages where he pleaded with people to give themselves to Jesus.

In 1846, the year after Newman joined the Roman Catholic Church, some thought Pusey might follow his friend. On Christmas Day, Pusey visited Bristol and preached in Clifton Parish Church. One who was present recorded,

> Never before did I hear so beautifully Evangelical a sermon as this from the man who has given a name to a party which is supposed to represent a different principle in the Church . . . He was listened to throughout by that little crowded church with fixed and rapt attention, though it was neither declamatory, noisy, nor eccentric; but plaintive, solemn, and subdued, breathing throughout, I may say, a beauty of holiness and a Christian spirit so broad and Catholic, so deep and devotional, that while the most zealous Protestant could find nothing in it he might not approve, the most bigoted Roman Catholic could not enter an exception to a single expression it contained.

At the end of the service, the same correspondent heard an exchange between two Bristol girls as they left the church.

'Who be that that preached?' said one. 'A monstrous nice man, but dreadful long.'

'Don't you know?' replied the other. 'It's that Mr Pusey, who's such a friend to the Pope. But come along, or we'll be late for tea!'

Twenty-nine years later, the 'monstrous nice man' was still very much an Anglican and still 'dreadful long'. During the 1850s and '60s, absurd stories were told about him and some wags maintained that he sacrificed a lamb every Friday – though by many he was viewed with a mixture of suspicion, respect and affection. None of the attacks and misrepresentations ever soured him or made him bitter. Undeterred by Isaac Williams's warnings about attaching too much importance to preaching, Pusey would frequently preach for an hour.

On Septuagesima Sunday, 1875, when he was seventy-five, still the Regius Professor of Hebrew, still a canon of Christ Church, he preached before the university in Newman's old pulpit in St Mary's. His text was the words of Jesus in Luke 9:23: 'If anyone would come after me, he must deny himself and take up his cross daily and follow me.' At almost the end of an hour's sermon, he looked up at the rows of prosperous-looking undergraduates sitting in the gallery.

'Many of you, my sons,' he told them, 'are provided with superfluities. You have not to stint yourselves as to the pleasures of your age. Day by day passes, I suppose, with all conveniences of life or amusement, or some self-indulgences which, though not directly sinful, are rather injurious. If our Lord was to come now, in how many do you think that you could tell Him that you had fed Him, clothed Him, supplied Him when sick? Some, I fear, could not say that they had bestowed as much on Christ as upon their dogs . . .

'He does not put hard things upon you. He Who accepts the cup of cold water will accept petty self-denials. Self-indulgence is a hard master – not Jesus. Vice wears the body; self-denial braces it. Sin is an exacting tyrant: the service of God is perfect freedom.

'Give yourselves anew to Him, Who gave Himself for you. He grudged not for you one drop of His heart's blood; grudge not to Him the price of His blood – yourselves. Think of that place around the eternal throne which He by that blood has individually prepared for you. Jesus will impart to your petty cross some of the virtue of His saving cross. He will make any hardness sweet to you, Who is Himself all sweetness, and every pleasurable delight.'

In his *Short History of the Oxford Movement*, first published in 1915, Dr S. L. Ollard wrote that the movement

> began, continued, and is today a strenuous attempt to preach Jesus Christ as for many years He had not been preached in England. The popular Evangelical theology laid stress on the work of Christ for us; the men of the Oxford Movement preached Him as a living Master who could teach now as well as save. It enforced self-discipline, a hardness with self, often austerity; it inspired in its followers a hatred of shams and pretence and unreality in religion, it made men distrust their feelings.

Of all the writers of the *Tracts for the Times*, only one (Newman) became a Roman Catholic. The rest died as they had lived, faithful servants of the Church of England. 'The moral beauty of the Tractarians,' Ollard wrote, 'showed itself in their faces. In few other collections of portraits is there such distinction of form and beauty of feature as in the portraits of the men of the Oxford Movement.'

As a result of the movement's teaching and writing, Anglican worship underwent a transformation. Holy Communion was restored to an increasingly central place; there was a renewed appreciation of the beauty of liturgy and a demand for both richer forms and more ceremonial expression. The pattern of prayer in the daily office grew to be widely observed among the clergy. There was a revival of sacramental confession and of the religious life. A new openness to Roman Catholicism and Eastern Orthodoxy led to a growing search for Christian unity. The Anglo-Catholic congresses in the inter-war years indicated the growing strength of the Oxford Movement tradition, but perhaps it would be fair to say that in the second half of the twentieth century Evangelicalism has been in the ascendancy within the Church of England. However, today as in the 1830s,

Anglo-Catholics and Evangelicals often recognise how much they have in common, in their opposition to liberalism and their concern for a religion of the heart.

31 I have another dream

As I recall the reaction to Pusey's sermon in Clifton Parish Church, I have another dream, though I am wide awake as I put it on paper. The starting point of this dream is the Bristolian who listened to Pusey preach and declared that he heard nothing which a Protestant might not approve nor a Catholic take exception. It takes up the thought that the Oxford Movement was a revival given its spirit by Evangelicalism and its form by Catholicism. In this dream I see that while every label, except perhaps that of Christian, is unsatisfactory, we have to live with them and that the Christian Church is currently stuck with four in particular: Evangelical, Charismatic, Catholic and Liberal. Many Christians would be happy to accept more than one of these labels for themselves, some even all four and some none.

My dream is that Evangelicals, Charismatics and Catholics will recognise that the things they have in common are far greater than the things which divide them. By Catholics, I do not of course mean just Roman Catholics, but those within the Church of England and other denominations who gladly see themselves as members of the Holy Catholic Church. Here are eight strands which I think should unite Evangelicals, Charismatics and Catholics.

First, they take their religion seriously. Their Christian faith is not a hobby tagged on the end of a list of other interests: it dominates their lives.

Second, Evangelicals, Charismatics and Catholics love Jesus intensely as Lord and Saviour, whether they express this love singing Graham Kendrick worship choruses, in their prayer meetings, their quiet times with God or in their sacramental life. In these times they will celebrate the gospel truth that God's amazing grace is offered to us freely through Christ.

Third, Evangelicals, Charismatics and Catholics have, as Pusey put it, a 'zeal for souls'. Even the most extreme supporter of the Oxford Movement, William Ward, said that the Christian Church must always be on the look-out for the conversion of souls; Newman said that true preaching of the gospel is to preach Christ; Isaac Williams said that the whole business of the Church was to impart to men and women true saving knowledge. More recently, Clifford Longley described the present Pope as an 'Evangelical Roman Catholic, if such a thing exists, in that he believes in going after people, warming their hearts and converting them'.[6] It is to the credit of Evangelicals and Charismatics that I don't need to begin quoting Billy Graham, David Watson or John Stott to prove their zeal for souls.

Fourth, Evangelicals, Charismatics and Catholics love the Scriptures. Newman recalled that he was brought up to delight in his Bible and retained this all his life, even when he came to the view that the Scriptures can disappoint and prove divisive unless approached with the humility which respects the teaching of the universal Church helping us interpret the mind of God.

Fifth, Evangelicals, Charismatics and Catholics earnestly pursue holiness remembering the words of God, 'Be holy, because I am holy' (1 Pet. 1:15). They recognise the danger that a belief either in justification by faith or baptismal regeneration can be held negatively so as to lower the importance of pursuing holiness. 'Both doctrines,' said Pusey, 'may be abused to our destruction.' They will recognise that a presentation of the gospel which amounts to little more than 'Come to Jesus. Trust in Him. Your problems will disappear' is less than the truth. Evangelicals, Charismatics and Catholics take seriously the advice of the Apostle Peter to 'make every effort to add to your faith goodness; and to goodness, knowledge; and to knowledge, self-control; and to self-control, perseverance; and to perseverance, godliness; and to godliness, brotherly kindness; and to brotherly kindness, love' (2 Pet. 1:5–7).

Sixth, Evangelicals and Catholics will surely want to agree with Charismatics that, as Newman put it, whatever is done in the Christian Church is done by the Holy Spirit. Whatever else we may say about the Holy Spirit, we will surely all want to agree with Newman that the presence of the Holy Spirit in our hearts, the author both of faith and renewal, is really that which makes us righteous: that our righteousness is the possession of that presence. The Holy Spirit is given to every Christian to produce renovation and justification. Justification is a real and actual communication to the soul of the atonement through the work and presence of the Holy Spirit. In saying this, Newman anticipated the work of theologians in this century who have been working to produce joint statements on behalf of Anglicans and Roman Catholics.

Seventh, Evangelicals, Charismatics and Catholics recognise that while every Christian leader wants to fill his Church, his message will include an element of severity as well as comfort. They recall the disconcerting words of Jesus that, 'Not everyone who says to me, "Lord, Lord," will enter the kingdom of heaven, but only he who does the will of my Father who is in heaven. Many will say to me on that day, "Lord, Lord, did we not prophesy in your name, and in your name drive out demons and perform many miracles?" Then I will tell them plainly, "I never knew you. Away from me, you evildoers!"' (Matt. 7:21–3). They will agree with Isaac Williams that obedience is the biblical means of promoting Christianity in the world and with Newman that *the cross* is both the challenge to be taken up by the true disciple and the measure of every expression of Christianity. Like William Ward, they will take sin seriously, recognising that sin is more of an enemy to be feared than self-righteousness.

They will recognise that judgment to come is an integral part of Christian doctrine and will be suspicious of theories which soften the impact of this truth.

And the final strand is that for Evangelicals, Charismatics and Catholics the Christian life must be real. It's for this reason that Newman's writings have come to be loved by non-Catholics as well as Catholics: to him, the only argument for Christianity that proves anything is that it works, that it actually changes people. Christianity is far more than a cold system of dogma, empty phrases, pious platitudes: it's the way of the cross, of self-denial, death to self and rising again to a new life of faith and joyous obedience.

In my dream I see in these eight strands a sacred common ground of truth on the basis of which many of us from different traditions can walk together as we approach the dawn of a new century, thinking of each other as 'not strangers but pilgrims'.

Preaching in Lincoln Cathedral on the Eve of St Peter's Day 1972, Archbishop Michael Ramsey chose as his text these words of Peter: 'As you come to him, the living Stone – rejected by men but chosen by God and precious to him – you also, like living stones, are being built into a spiritual house' (1 Pet. 2:4–5a). Standing in the midst of the stones of the lovely Minster, he shared his dream of the Church: I see a community of Christians conscious of being called apart in the way of holiness, but never self-conscious as their awareness is of the God whom they worship and the people whom they serve and care for. I see such a community ardently devoted to the worship of God in a worship where awe and beauty and mystery are mingled with homeliness and fellowship. I see such a community practising fellowship amongst themselves as the walls of denominations yield to the discovery of unity in Christ's truth . . . I see such a community full of active compassion for the poor, the homeless, the hungry and lonely.'

In this Decade of Evangelism, may we not on this basis

more effectively carry out our Saviour's parting commission to 'go and make disciples of all nations, baptising them in the name of the Father and of the Son and of the Holy Spirit, and teaching them to obey everything I have commanded you'? If so, may Christ's related promise give us renewed strength in the task: 'And surely I am with you always, to the very end of the age' (Matt. 28:19–20).

Endnotes

1 See A. .M. Allchin in his introduction to the 1963 edition of Ollard's *Short History of the Oxford Movement*.
2 In addition to the extract from Stott's *The Message of the Sermon on the Mount*, already quoted, see J. N. D. Anderson, *Morality, Law and Grace*.
3 *Stepping Stones: Joint Essays on Anglican Catholic and Evangelical Unity*.
4 Inter-Anglican Theological and Doctrinal Commission, *For the Sake of the Kingdom: God's Church and the New Creation*, p. 23.
5 Quoted in *Stepping Stones*.
6 *The Times*, May 30th, 1992.

Principal sources used

J. N. D. Anderson, *Morality, Law and Grace*, London, 1972
R. H. Bainton, *Here I Stand: A Life of Martin Luther*, New York, 1950
O. Chadwick, *The Mind of the Oxford Movement*, London, 1960
O. Chadwick, *The Spirit of the Oxford Movement*, London, 1990
O. Chadwick, *Newman, Past Masters, Oxford*, 1983
O. Chadwick, *The Victorian Church*, part I, third edition, London, 1966

R. W. Church, *The Oxford Movement, 1833–1845*, London, 1891

A Dictionary of Christian Spirituality, edited by Gordon S. Wakefield, London, 1983

V. H. H. Green, *The University Church of St Mary the Virgin, Oxford*, London, 1975

L. I. Guiney, *Hurrell Froude: Memoranda and Comments*, London, 1904

Inter-Anglican Theological and Doctrinal Commission, *For the Sake of the Kingdom: God's Church and the New Creation*, London, 1986

I. Kerr, *John Henry Newman*, Oxford, 1990

H. P. Liddon, *Life of E. B. Pusey*, vols 1–4, London, 1898

W. Lock, *John Keble*, London, 1893

T. Mozley, *Reminiscences; chiefly of Oriel College and the Oxford Movement*, London, 1882

New Dictionary of Theology, Leicester, 1988

Newman's Oxford: A Guide to Pilgrims, Oxford, 1966

J. H. Newman, *Apologia Vita Sua*, edited by Maisie Ward, 1945

J. H. Newman, *Lectures on Justification*, London, 1838

J. H. Newman, *Parochial and Plain Sermons*, London, 1878

S. L. Ollard, *A Short History of the Oxford Movement*, 150th Anniversary Oxford Movement Edition, London, 1963

J. Pollock, *John Wesley*, London, 1989

E. B. Pusey, *The Church of England a Portion of Christ's one Holy Catholic Church, and a means of restoring visible unity. An Eirenicon, in a letter to the author of 'The Christian Year'*, London, 1865

J. H. Overton, *John Wesley*, Oxford, 1891

G. W. E. Russell, *The Household of Faith*, London, 1913

A. P. Stanley, *Life of Thomas Arnold*, London, 1904

J.R.W. Stott, *The Message of the Sermon on the Mount*, Leicester, 1978

J. R. W. Stott, and R. Greenacre, *Stepping Stones: Joint Essays on Anglican Catholic and Evangelical Unity*, London, 1987

Tracts for the Times, vols I–V, London, 1833–1840

M. Ward, *Young Mr Newman*, London, 1952

W. Ward, *The Life of John Henry, Cardinal Newman*, 2 vols, London, 1912

W. Ward, *W. G. Ward and the Oxford Movement*, London, 1889